FISHER'S CONCISE HISTORY OF ECONOMIC BUNGLING

FISHER'S CONCISE HISTORY OF ECONOMIC BUNGLING

A Guide for Today's Statesmen

ANTONY FISHER

CAROLINE HOUSE BOOKS • OTTAWA, ILLINOIS

Previously published in the
United Kingdom under the title
Must History Repeat Itself?
by Churchill Press Limited
©A.G.A. Fisher 1974
Revised Edition ©1978
A.G.A. Fisher

This edition has been published as part of the
publishing program of Liberty Fund, Inc.
Liberty Fund is a foundation established to
encourage study of the ideal of a society of free
and responsible individuals.

ISBN: 0-916054-63-2 clothbound
ISBN: 0-916054-69-1 paperbound

Library of Congress Catalogue Card Number 77-15916

Manufactured in the United States of America

Caroline House Books/Green Hill Publishers, Inc., Ottawa, Illinois 61350

Dedicated to my brother, Basil

"They shall grow not old, as we that are left grow old;
Age shall not weary them, nor the years condemn.
At the going down of the sun and in the morning
We will remember them."

LAURENCE BINYON

Contents

Acknowledgments

This book grew out of my efforts over more than a decade to compile evidence to show the difference between what I have more and more come to see as the right and wrong approaches of governments through the ages to "solve" economic and social problems. From extensive reading, discussion, travel, and varied business experience, I found no difficulty in assembling many historical examples, quotations, and experiences. Indeed, the growing bulk became so large that it was doubtful whether it could all go into one book.

What decided me to stop writing and start looking for a publisher was the almost uncanny way events began to bear out the warnings I have for years been making privately as a result of this study of history. Lacking experience in authorship, I therefore appealed to John Wood and Dr. Rhodes Boyson for help in severely reducing to a manageable length a bulky manuscript that had "just growed" like Topsy over more than ten years. After major surgery on the text, Ralph Harris undertook the difficult task of refining it into a form suitable for publication. For these three friends I have the greatest respect and warmest gratitude.

From many others to whom I am indebted for assistance at various stages, I must single out Sudha Shenoy who helped in research and checking and Joy Northey, my secretary for many years, who has typed and retyped material running to a length many times greater than appears here.

There are many colleagues in my business ventures and personal friends in America as well as England who have taught me much that I try to apply in this book. But above all I must express my debt to Professor F. A. Hayek who inspired my original interest in economic research almost thirty years ago and who has ever since encouraged me by his example and teachings to hold firm to the faith that it is the battle of ideas which will decide the future prospects of a free society.

A.G.A.F.

Introduction

Even the most cursory study of the history of the human race provides evidence of constant human failure, leading to violence and man's inhumanity to man. Those who have lived through the most recent expressions of this violence—the Second World War, the wars in Korea and Vietnam, the Castro Revolution, the Russian invasions of Hungary and Czechoslovakia, and the Chinese purges—will know something of the stress, the pain, the fear, and the hysteria that such devastating explosions produce in man.

On the Sunday nearest to November 11 each year memorial services to the dead of the two great wars are held in many countries. But these memorial services, together with the many statues and plaques dedicated "in lasting memory" to those who have given their lives, regrettably do little or nothing to prevent similar ghastly events in the future. Memories, and even memorials, fade as the unsolved problems of the past simply take on slightly new forms.

Back to first principles

As I relate in the pages that follow, there is sufficient similarity between unhappy developments in history to challenge our intellectual abilities to explain what keeps going wrong. This book is my effort to meet that challenge.

In Chapter 1, I study three possible explanations of why things go wrong. The first is that everything which happens is a matter of random chance. Existence itself would then be no more than the spinning of an infinite number of roulette wheels supported by an infinite number of games. But as Einstein once wrote: "I cannot believe that God plays dice with the world."

A second possibility is that on countless occasions throughout history a few evil men have acquired the understanding and power to trick the vast majority of mankind into conditions of misery or slavery using coercion, revolution, and even war to that end.

A third possibility is that some natural order exists in the form of an infinite variety of cause-and-effect relationships, but that we do not yet understand them sufficiently to run our affairs harmoniously. It would follow that the economic and social disasters which continually overwhelm us come about, not only because we are unaware of these relationships but also because we are almost certainly unaware that any such principles could exist. If this latter proposition is true, it is possible to make sense of man's recurring disasters. History and modern experience would then fit into place and point inexorably to further periods of misery and chaos unless cause and effect are correctly understood and applied.

In Chapter 2, therefore, I go on to offer a more detailed study of cause-and-effect relationships, explaining how man's troubles could have arisen because he himself has been ignorant of their existence. One major problem is that, like the principle of gravity, the many forces acting on each of us as individuals are invisible and intangible while only the consequences are discernible to man's physical senses. I then try to show how the understanding of cause-and-effect relationships can have tremendous consequences. Quite contrary to general opinion, the politician whose duty it is to create new laws or change old laws is seldom, if ever, an originator. Nor are the communications media usually the prime mover. Neither the politician nor the journalist has time enough for thought or research, and both inevitably become immersed in compromise and short-term calculations. I give reasons for thinking that new understanding has to come from independent individuals who can give sufficient time to intellectual study.

Letting history speak

Chapter 3 dips into history over a period of almost five thousand years. There is much evidence that wars, started for various reasons, regularly result in the creation of bureaucracies and taxes. When the wars are over, the bureaucracies and the taxes increase rather than decrease, which in turn creates inflationary conditions. Again and again governments then attempt to hold down wages and prices by law without solving the problem.

History also provides evidence that where governments have pursued the opposite policy of maximizing individual choice within a framework of law and moral conduct, their problems have given way to prosperity. Hence my conviction that history does teach lessons, provided that the past experience of mankind can be studied in the light of what I call cause-and-effect relationships or others may describe as principles.

I owe an explanation to the reader for the many quotations, particularly in Chapter 3. Because I am not an historian, I have thought it more appropriate to rely on original quotations which I believe give the argument more strength than I could give it in my own words.

In Chapter 4, I apply the same basic thinking to more recent experience. Examples are drawn from agriculture both within the United Kingdom and elsewhere, and from industry and commerce throughout the world, to illustrate that success or failure of government policies does depend on the application of right principles. In Chapter 5, I produce evidence for my conviction that theoretical study does yield practical consequences. I offer examples from my own experience that documented understanding, even by one person, can suffice to move government to make correct policy decisions. The essential ingredient is deep understanding, which in turn can be achieved only by dedicated concentration and research.

Chapter 6 is my attempt to document the final stage in this analysis by proposing actions which the government must take to produce the benefits that have been sought by many and have evaded all. Among the consequences of policies deliberately intended to maximize individual choice will be low taxation and a maximum increase in the wealth of the poorer members of the community.

In this way I put my own theories to the test. I believe that it is hardly possible to say or write anything that has not been said or written before. But what I have gathered together may be written in a way that is new. I have tried to unite the various arguments and contentions in a continuous whole leading to clear conclusions which have been incorporated in what politicians might call a manifesto. If I am right it will have inevitable consequences, possibly more quickly than anybody dare hope.

I wrote most of the book in 1969 and 1970. After much condensation and editing, *Must History Repeat Itself?* was published in Great Britain in 1974. Even then, some of my predictions were overtaken by events.

This North American edition of 1978 has been generally updated. Material that was of interest only to Britons, such as the specific reforms necessary for the revival of that nation's economy, have been cut out, while new material of general interest has been added. In the final chapter I offer some new guidelines for resolving the dilemmas of inflation and stagnation that afflict the West. I no longer believe reform can be a ten-year process; it must happen quickly if it is to be done at all.

A personal note

My father was killed in the First World War in 1917. My only brother, Basil, was killed flying a Hurricane in the Battle of Britain on August 15, 1940. He, our common friend David Berry, and I were members of 111 Hurricane Squadron. David Berry, for whom I had great respect, was killed flying his Hurricane over France even before the Battle of Britain commenced. I survived but with no thanks to my own efforts, for it was some time before I was to learn that the main ability for which I and my squadron existed, to destroy enemy aircraft, was an ability I did not possess. Unaware of my inability, and maybe with a less than average inclination for violent aggression, I was no credit in that particular occupation.

Later I was to learn the great difficulty, even with eight machine-guns, of hitting an enemy plane. Yet as soon as I became aware of that difficulty, I became a more useful Royal Air Force officer. That tale is not for telling here; the point I wish to underline is that only when I became aware of an inability was I able to set about correcting it. From that moment I hope I became an asset and no longer a liability. I discovered that I was not the only fighter pilot who had been unaware of the great difficulty of hitting an enemy plane, or of the need for technical and strategic efficiency to fulfil the purpose a fighter pilot was expected to achieve. I learned that good intentions were not enough.

In the pages that follow I offer evidence which has convinced me that mankind is in much the same position as I was as an ignorant fighter pilot and in worse danger for being unaware of the need to correct that ignorance.

It must be true that any successful effort to achieve better understanding of the motives and behavior of communities is a more enduring memorial to those who gave their lives for peace than any memorial in stone. Many have tried to add another rung to man's ladder of understanding. I offer the following pages as my own endeavor.

1
Think It Out
THE ROLE OF PRINCIPLES

As we move into the late 70s, people in the West are richer than they have ever been before—and this is probably also true of the people of the East. Despite the increase in material wealth since the last war, the process looks increasingly precarious. This book is written in the belief that history has started to repeat itself in the sense that current developments are not all progress and may be downhill. My argument will be that economic progress stems from an appropriate form of government and that, more recently, growth has been despite—and not because of—our present form of government.

Familiar symptoms

Are we not trying to grapple with something which might be likened to a disease? Some politicians and journalists argue that what is happening is "progress." But that should lead to prosperity, happiness, and a better life, whereas the trends that worry me point in the opposite direction. The following is a grim list of clearly discernible and recurring ingredients of the syndrome which threatens us:

(a) a steady decrease in the freedom of choice available to the individual;

(b) a steady increase in taxes;

(c) a steady increase in the number of central and local civil servants;

(d) an extension of state ownership, often called "nationalization," done sometimes to help firms and industries out of trouble;

(e)   an accelerating decrease in the value of money, resulting in a continuing increase in prices;

(f)   an increasing resistance to taxation through various forms of evasion;

(g)   increasing discontent expressed particularly in industrial action, student unrest, and civil disobedience;

(h)   the fixing of wages and prices;

(i)   a growing "black market" in wages and the use of money;

(j)   a tendency to ascribe any apparent benefits to state action, and to blame difficulties on individuals as "strikers," "profiteers," "landlords," "speculators";

(k)   a weakening of the rule of law and the protection of the individual by the state, which curtails rather than preserves personal rights;

(l)   a steady deterioration in moral standards.

These symptoms affect every individual. They reflect the failure of particular policies. If I am right, and if standards of living appear to be rising while the undertow of decline is developing, any improvement comes about *despite* government interference with the economy and not because of it. But in fact living standards in Great Britain appear now to be in a state of chronic decline. The *Daily Telegraph* of Oct. 10, 1975, reported that between March and June of that year, living standards dropped by between 2.5 and 3 per cent.

As we will see, history provides much evidence that as the economic disease progresses, a familiar result has been the establishment of tyranny or dictatorship, when the state and its public functionaries become all-powerful. Government becomes a Frankenstein's Monster, "a thing which gets out of the control of its creator." During recent centuries, one of the main objects of government has been to prevent any private individual or group from obtaining too much power but, unless checks are established, there is a natural temptation for government to end up taking too much power for itself.

Since increasing government power reduces individual freedom, a point is reached when people feel driven to resist, even at the risk of disorder and sometimes revolution.

The source of wealth

Some civilizations have been more successful than others, but there have been fewer periods of progress than of stagnation, retrogression and destruction. Such ebbing and flowing in the tides of human civilization have been caused less by the vagaries of nature than by decisions made by men themselves.

It may seem obvious that the wealth of nations which are relatively rich and provide wider choices for their citizens, has come about because they owned abundant natural resources. Yet both China and Russia own tremendous quantities of valuable assets in the form of land and minerals but are pathetically poor compared with the U.S.A. or most European nations. The Venetians built up an empire without any resources and, indeed, probably developed their trading ability *because* they had no other resources. The Swiss have one of the strongest currencies in the world, but it is not backed by physical resources. Hong Kong, in recent years, has also shown itself a remarkable creator of wealth under the most unlikely circumstances. An overpopulated rock without even a water supply has become first a trading center and then a manufacturing challenger to better-endowed nations.

It is plain that the wealth of nations develops from other factors than merely the natural resources available. It may even be argued that physical advantages remove the need to compete through innovation.

Do we need theory?

Economics is the study of man's decision-making in the use of scarce resources. Although it governs a large part of human action, its study is apt to bewilder people, if it does not frighten them off.

If we wish to build houses, we study architecture. If we wish to build bridges or power stations, we study engineering and physics. If we wish to fly to the moon, we have to study many sciences, including physics, chemistry, and advanced mathematics. In such activities, the experts can agree sufficiently to avoid frequent failure. Yet when we consult economists, we find they disagree on almost every practical issue. My case here is that unless we can understand the central principles of economics the practical consequences will become increasingly unpleasant.

Although governments are nowadays guided by "economists," they are as wanderers in a desert without a compass, without knowledge of the stars, without maps, or, worse still, with faulty instruments and inaccurate maps. The more surely human beings have been able to establish given relationships between cause and consequence in mathematics, physics, and chemistry, the more surely have veritable miracles of scientific progress been achieved. The study of economics has certainly lagged far behind.

Newton and Einstein

Not surprisingly, successful businessmen often scorn economists and go on to doubt the value of any kind of economic theory. Yet, as in the physical sciences, correct theory must come before effective action. Of course, theories can be right or wrong and will have corresponding consequences. The problem is not whether to employ theory, but how to distinguish good from bad theories.

Newton was the first to discover and relate the laws of gravity and motion in such a way that theory became a practical guide to action so that the relationship between cause and effect could be used to achieve predictable results. It would have been impossible to land men on the moon and return them to earth without first understanding a great deal of theory.

One big difficulty in understanding theories about economic forces is that they are intangible. To understand them it is necessary to use our mental capacity and for this reason these forces seem quite unreal to many people. Nevertheless they are extraordinarily powerful and sure achievement depends on our precise understanding of them. Deciding economic policy without discovery of the correct theory is action without thought, which is not only wasteful but dangerous.

Even where politicians or their advisers do give time to thinking, their final policies have increasingly come to be based on a large measure of compromise or consensus; that is, on a mixture of true and false theories. Imagine trying to land men on the moon by a compromise of conflicting theories!

In order to simplify the discussion, I shall use the word *principle* to refer to a basic assumption or a relationship between a cause and its effect.[1] In trying to study the consequences and the causes of government action, I am searching for economic principles which will achieve the desired ends in the most effective way. It is important not to confuse man-made laws with natural laws, such as gravity, which will function and produce their consequences whatever man may or may not know and think about them. Since man-made laws do not assume there are principles on which legislation should be based, it is not surprising they produce disturbing, if not disastrous consequences despite well-intentioned and desirable aims.

One classic example of the consequences of the understanding of correct theory is that of Einstein, whose perception of physics and mathematics was such that he was able theoretically to work out a formula which is expressed as $E=MC^2$ and which has revolutionized our sources of energy. Today no military leader can disregard the consequences that have arisen from Einstein's understanding of powerful forces. Einstein's theories are very "practical" in that they have had physical consequences which can be predetermined and created at will. In 1938 Einstein wrote a letter to President Roosevelt suggesting that he investigate the possibility of producing an atom bomb. That letter made it impossible for either the Germans or the Japanese to win the war. How potent can be the power of understanding of only one man!

Six ways of deciding

Some readers will no doubt be thinking that theory and principles may have their place in the physical world but that they cannot apply to man's activities. One assumption is that economics is a consequence of human decision-making which is itself unpredictable. It may appear reasonable to assume that since the individual is free to make up his mind, and since therefore he has wide choice in what actions he may take, there can be no predetermined relationship between economic cause and economic consequence. The purpose of this study of theory, history, and modern experience is to give reasons for thinking there is such a relationship. If there is and we can discover it, we can avoid the mistakes made in the past. If there is no such relationship, our trials and tribulations have come about by chance and not from any particular cause which might be avoided in the future—a dismal prospect indeed.

If economics is about the use of scarce resources, it must study human decision-making. Every decision must be motivated by the intention to produce a desired consequence. There would appear to be some six main methods of making decisions. These are in ascending order of reliability: superstition, wrong assumption, guessing, experiment, experience, and finally the scientific method when a known cause-and-effect relationship is completely understood. It is also true that decisions can be guided by instinct, emotion, dogma, and religion, but I consider each of these may fit into the six main categories, or are substitutes for conscious decision-making. Let us look at the main methods by which human beings make their decisions, starting with the most effective, namely the scientific method.

The *Oxford Dictionary* defines science in part as

> a branch of study which is concerned either with a connected body of demonstrated truths or with observed facts systematically classified and more or less collated by being brought under general laws and which includes trustworthy methods of the discovery of new truths within its own domain.

The study of physics can therefore be described as a science and the law of gravity as one of the principles on which this science is based. Scientific understanding can be applied to many decisions to achieve sure results, but for most decision-making science is not available and we have to use other methods. The next method most likely to provide sure results is experience. For some things that we do, we have learned from experience or have been taught by others how best to achieve them. The lessons of experience have to be adapted to changing circumstances but, where we have appropriate experience, the element of chance in the achievement of our aims is reduced. Education in school is partly an attempt by society to help the coming generations benefit from past experience.

But if neither science nor experience is available, the next most economical method for achieving a given end is experimentation. An experiment can be designed to test various methods and to find out which produces the desired consequences at the lowest cost. To experiment can be expensive where there are many alternative hypotheses to test, but often it is the cheapest method available. Much human effort is expended in the form of experimentation and often there is no other way.

Thus we have three more or less rational methods for making decisions. Experiment and experience are less effective than scientific theory but have to be used when it is not available. If none of these rational methods is possible, we are left with guessing or superstition, which may be dignified with the description of "wrong assumption." The guessing process may be bolstered by dogma, fashion, instinct, or emotion but the chance of success is nothing like fifty-fifty where there may be dozens or hundreds of alternative wrong decisions and only a single right one.

The least satisfactory method of all for achieving decision-making must be superstition or wrong assumption. If guessing is hazardous with little chance of producing the right answer, superstition is even more certain to produce the wrong answers. History is full of examples of decisions made for superstitious reasons. Endlessly, Roman emperors and generals and lesser folk relied on a "religion" which was based on superstition. Millions of animals and humans must have been sacrificed over the centuries in this wasteful effort.

Where Marx was wrong . . .

As an example of an influential principle, let us examine Karl Marx's basic assumption that work creates wealth.

> A use value or useful article therefore has value because human labor in the abstract has been embodied or materialized in it . . . How then is the magnitude of this value to be measured? Plainly, by the quantity of the value-creating substance of the labor contained in the article. The quantity of labor, however, is measured by its duration, and labor-time in its turn finds its standards in weeks, days, and years . . . We see then that that which determines the magnitude of the value of any article is the amount of labor socially necessary or the labor-time socially necessary for its production.[2]

Marx thus argued that the real value of anything is made up of the labor time put into it. In the passages quoted he used the words "socially necessary" because he realized that the exchange values of two articles may be quite different from their respective costs. Nevertheless, since his conclusions would break down completely if he could not prove that wealth is always necessarily created by work, he adopted the labor theory of value. If wealth is always created by work, and if the owner of a factory such as a shareholder does no work, he must be stealing from the workers when he takes profits. I am concerned here to show that Marx realized that he must start from some basic assumption, and this was his basic assumption or "principle." But, work does not *always* create wealth and the consequences of his theory when applied have been disastrous. Nevertheless Marxist theory was and is acclaimed as "scientific."

However, Marx's basic assumption is one with which many people agree, that work produces results assumed to be necessarily good. For instance, it is said of the Germans that they work harder than the British and therefore their economy is in a sounder state. Yet in the 1970s the amount of physical effort being expended by Russians, Chinese, or Indians may be much greater than that expended by the Germans, the Swiss, or the Americans. It is plainly not a question of how much work is done, but of how *effective* that particular work is in achieving its given ends, which we would take as being able to satisfy the customer who will pay no more than the product is worth to him. All who agree with Adam Smith's central dictum that "consumption is the sole end and purpose of all production" must accept that it is demand, not cost, which determines relative values.

. . . and Adam Smith was right

When we turn our attention to the consumer, it would seem obvious that the more an individual can satisfy his choices, the richer he will be. In the 20th century more people on the face of this earth have more choices and a larger ability to satisfy them than in any previous age. Why is this so? Adam Smith, again, tells us:

> This division of labor, from which so many advantages are derived, is not originally the effect of any human wisdom, which foresees and intends that general opulence to which it gives occasion. It is the necessary, though very slow and gradual, consequence of a certain propensity in human nature which has in view no such extensive utility: the propensity to truck, barter and exchange one thing for another. . . .
>
> *Whether this propensity be one of those original principles* in human nature, of which no further account can be given; or whether, as seems more probable, it be the necessary consequence of the faculties of reason and speech, it belongs not to our present subject to enquire. . . .[3] [My emphasis.]

It is my purpose here to study the possibility that voluntary exchange is a fundamental principle. Adam Smith also wrote:

> The uniform, constant and uninterrupted effort of every man to better his condition, the principle from which public and national, as well as private opulence is originally derived, is frequently powerful enough to maintain the natural progress of things towards improvement, in spite of both the extravagance of government and of the greatest errors of administration. . . . [4]

If we are to better our condition, we must be free to make the best use of our own efforts, to produce what *others* will want and to spend the proceeds on the products of others that satisfy us most. Every voluntary transaction is intended to be to the mutual benefit of both buyer and seller since one or other would soon withdraw if he found the exchange did not better his condition.

When asked by a disciple if there were one single word which could serve as a principle of conduct for life, Confucius[5] replied, "Perhaps the word *reciprocity* will do." May we interpret Confucius as agreeing that voluntary exchange is a principle?

When governments keep markets free, it becomes necessary for each producer to discover what services or products are most required and to produce them at least cost. Others will have to do likewise for their own requirements, thereby producing a division of labor which widens choice. Where all stand to gain from this widening of choice, we see the wealth-creating possibilities of reciprocity or voluntary exchange.[6] The more effective the division of labor, the stronger the demand for "protection" or "subsidy" by defenders of threatened interests whether manufacturers, farmers, or trade unions. The moment governments yield to such special pleading they embark on a descending spiral of diminishing choice for the generality of consumers.

Human beings often take a short view. They tend to see themselves as producers—workers, managers, investors—and fail to see that their interests as consumers are far more important to their economic welfare. The demand for government intervention invariably amounts to a call for politicians to protect everyone as a producer, against everybody as a consumer. Not only is this futile, it is a highly dangerous exercise setting up forces that can wreck society. Once again good intentions without understanding lead to opposite results from those intended.

So long as everyone exchanges that which he desires less for that which he desires more, the community must benefit. Voluntary exchange must be beneficial to both parties. It is the basis of profit and the creation of wealth. This communal or general increase in wealth as the result of exchange presupposes a framework of law and order which people are more likely to accept with honesty and integrity where everyone has a creative outlet for his natural effort to "better his condition."

Those who argue for free markets are often thought to be callous and uncaring about the poorer sections of the community. The truth is that the competitive system advocated by Adam Smith in practice enriches the choices *especially* of the less well-off, as Ludwig von Mises has explained:

> The characteristic feature of capitalism that distinguished it from precapitalistic methods of production was its new principles of marketing. Capitalism is not simply mass production, but *mass production to satisfy the needs of the masses*. The arts and crafts of the good old days catered almost exclusively to the wants of the well-to-do. But the factories produce cheap goods for the many. Big business, the target of fanatical hatred on the part of all contemporary governments and self-styled intellectuals, acquired and preserved its business only because it works for the masses.[7]

How much choice?

If it is true that the more there is voluntary exchange the richer the community will become, the duty of government must be to maximize individual choice. This does not mean either the permissive society or that everyone's choice can be unrestricted. Unlimited choice can be available only to a dictator who can gratify every whim at the expense of the choice of his subjects.

Nor is our goal the same as anarchy. Government and legislation are essential. A good example of "maximized choice" is the rule of the road which is a clearly accepted law enforcing a restriction applicable to *all* to keep to the right side. As a result the use of the road is maximized: so long as the rule applies to everyone equally, we avoid the "law of the jungle" where a person with a powerful vehicle or tank might do as he liked at our expense.

Legislation designed to maximize choice is legislation designed to protect equally all members of a nation or society and their property. It is legislation designed to facilitate exchanges and is not easy to devise. The first step is for legislators to be aware that they must make laws based on principles.

I hope I have set out enough of my thinking over many years to justify offering the following as a possible principle: people will make the best use of the scarce resources in a community, and thereby increase wealth fastest, where voluntary exchange is at a maximum. If this is so, a chief role of government is to maximize individual choice which leads to voluntary exchange.

It is probably true that most governments genuinely attempt to achieve policies that will produce desirable results. Many laws and policies assume that the best way to benefit the poorer sections of the community is at the expense of the richer who conveniently are in a minority as voters. But if the policies are wrong, if they are choice-reducing instead of choice-increasing, the consequences are made worse by further guessing, wrong assumptions, and compromise. Having reduced choice, governments all too readily reduce it further when the method employed inevitably does not produce the consequences hoped for. This step-by-step reduction in choice paves the way of Professor Hayek's "road to serfdom."[8]

If my basic principle of maximized choice for the individual is the key to growth and prosperity, the progressive reduction of choice at some stage leads inevitably to stagnation, confusion, disorder, and sometimes to chaos. I shall in later chapters apply this test to historical development and also to more recent events, both in Britain and elsewhere.

The competitive process

Before leaving theory, I wish to discover whether we need any other basic principles to guide economic policy. At least one is suggested by the requirement that to maximize choice government must ensure that markets are free, which means that competition prevails. Although competition can be painful for the less efficient or less competent, its vital importance is indicated by Professor Hayek who calls it "an optimum discovery procedure." This dictum is so important that it might be regarded as a secondary principle. After all, it would be difficult to deny the following sequence:

(i)   we are all imperfect in knowledge and ability;

(ii)   we will therefore always be making mistakes;

(iii)   there is no known perfect way of offering services or manufacturing products;

(iv)   in meeting change, competition provides a method of trial and error which is most likely to reveal the best solution.

From the manufacturer's point of view, comparison of his product with that of his competitors gives him a test of performance and impetus to improve the quality of his product. Without competition, a manufacturer would not possess a price indicator or profit-and-loss indicator. With the constant development of technology and changes in demand, there is no substitute for the discovery procedure of competition. It follows that monopoly which unavoidably reduces alternatives, especially "nationalization" which is state-protected monopoly, must be harmful.

Where competition is rigorous, the consumer will be offered better services or lower prices or both. He therefore controls the situation. Only the successful will make profits and they will be the measure of the success of any individual in serving the community. Losses will represent relative failure. From personal experience, I can confirm that if an individual is not operating under competitive conditions it is impossible to establish efficiency, or even to find out if an activity is making a profit or a loss.

Business v. bureaucracy

Man's own development over recorded history is the story of the competitive process summed up as the survival of the fittest. Animal life has been developing for some 650 million years and as new forms of life have occurred, so the stronger have squeezed out the weaker. An example of a species which for some reason or other failed to meet competition is the dodo. The phrase "as dead as the dodo" refers to the extinction of a bird which formerly flourished on the island of Mauritius in the Indian Ocean but which, having no predatory enemies, did not have to fly, and over the centuries forgot how to do so. When man and the dog first came to the island, the dodo could not compete and soon succumbed.

Where there are no competitive forces human beings, also, tend to take things easily. This situation is typified by a bureaucracy. Without any competitive check, government departments spend vast sums of money on services which the public would not choose to pay for voluntarily. One result is that governments are tempted to spend beyond their means and cover part of the cost by creating money, which incidentally, as we shall see, causes inflation. This is part of the syndrome of economic failure which can be traced back to the reduction of individual choice by policies that overrule voluntary exchange.

Business, which consists of an infinite variety of exchanges, cannot operate without honesty. The more complicated business becomes, the more necessary it is for honesty to prevail. Honesty is a form of certainty. It is apparent that the Quakers, who have a very strict code of honesty, played a major part in establishing the British joint stock banks. Was this a coincidence? These people trusted one another in a way that was possible for few others.

Successful endeavor, prosperity, "the better life" stem not only from honesty and free markets but also from conscientious effort. Successful effort in a competitive market must "care" about others. The same cannot be said of bureaucratic activity which by its nature limits a person's choice in spending a large part of his income.

I have argued that we cannot have a well-ordered, happy, compassionate, and advancing society without understanding basic principles which relate economic cause to consequence.

Can we learn to learn?

It would seem that as individuals we learn only as quickly as the cause of some consequence is made clear to us. Then, having learnt the cause of just that particular consequence, we can *act* accordingly to achieve the results—the consequence—we desire. This may be the achieving of a beneficial end or the avoiding of some undesirable end.

A small child learns to stand up straight at an early age. He does this because if he leans over, gravity pulls him to the ground. He does not learn about gravity, physics, Newton, or Einstein until much later, if ever. But the consequence of defying gravity is relayed to his mind almost instantaneously, so that his reaction is very quick and the learning process therefore rapid also.

But if we look at other cause-and-effect relationships, as for instance that consequence we call *inflation,* we find much confusion about the cause, much disagreement even about the consequence itself. Thus it is difficult to prevent the consequence. There is much, some would say overwhelming, evidence that inflation is the drop in the value of money or "promises to pay" made by government, which results when a government overissues the promises beyond its capacity to repay them. Several definitions of inflation are given, as well as other causes.

If we accept the first of these definitions, that if the government does print money excessively this does cause inflation, the effect will be to raise or to appear to raise prices of goods and services throughout the community using that particular money.

When the price of rice or butter rises then housewives are apt to criticize grocers. When workers ask for more pay to meet the higher prices, people blame the workers for asking too much pay, and blame the inflation upon them. The real cause is misguided government. Only government can correct the problem by altering its own policy, not anyone else's.

On countless occasions throughout history, such mistaken assumptions have been assumed to be correct. Then with the best intentions governments have acted upon them, attempting to hold down both prices and wages in various ways, which are always counterproductive, and often called wage and price controls. History is strewn with such attempts and also the consequences, always bad, but often disastrous. Thus in this example of inflation we find that the linkage between a consequence and its cause is not only very slow to appear but is illusory, and seems the reverse of the true cause. And so the wrong causes are blamed and the wrong remedies applied, thus making the consequences worse. Thus a community or nation, bewildered, anxious, and confused, blunders into trouble, if not disaster, as so many others have done before. Until we understand the problem we all are fated to repeat the same set of undesirable consequences.

There is much evidence that human beings in general do have good intentions but that their understanding does not match these good intentions.

My purpose is to explore a cause of the weakness in human ability to learn. People tend to be lazy and only when circumstances are such as to force them to think, do they stretch their minds. If people avoid thinking unless they have to, and therefore only too often learn, if at all, by chance, it must follow that in matters which we describe as being connected with economics or "human action" the ability to learn is not only very slow, but may be so twisted as to teach the wrong lessons. My purpose is to study the phenomenon to see if it exists, and if it does exist to discover ways of causing men to think before they have to.

Now we turn to some practical applications.

2
Write It Down
THE NEED TO DOCUMENT THE CASE

It is one thing to discuss the theories behind alternative policies, but it is also necessary to explain how they can be put into effect without getting bogged-down in party politics. The public's impression is that politics are at best a tiresome necessity. Politicians are generally assumed to be insincere, while compromise is probably accepted as a vocational hazard. Two hundred years ago, Adam Smith contrasted the ideal legislator "whose deliberations ought to be governed by general principles which are always the same" with "that insidious and crafty animal sometimes called a statesman or politician whose counsels are directed by the momentary fluctuations of affairs."

If my contention is true that government policy-making is based on ignorance, or at best on guesswork, a change in government is unlikely to provide lasting relief to our trials. The ship of state is like a raft being swept towards the rapids, and an election merely brings the prospect of somebody else's hand on the tiller. If economic salvation depended only on a change of party in power, Britain should surely be in economic heaven already. Mr. Wilson's "100 days" in 1964-5 was supposed to bring perfection in place of "thirteen years of Tory misrule." The practical result was that all our difficulties were made worse.

One more plan

Lord George-Brown, like countless politicians before him, thought he had only to make a plan and all would be well. It is unlikely he was aware of previous similar attempts: few politicians realize there is almost nothing they can do which has not already been tried time and again. Despite Lord George-Brown's obvious sincerity and wish to do good, the effort exploded in his face because he did not understand what he was doing.

In May 1965, four months *before* the publication of *The National Plan,* the Institute of Economic Affairs published an Eaton Paper with the same title in which John Brunner unerringly pointed to its practical futility as a "vague indication of aspirations." In the event, the National Plan for 1964 to 1970 was published in September 1965, with heavy emphasis that it had been prepared "in cooperation with private and nationalized industries." Nine months later the Labor Government abandoned it in favor of an unplanned package of crisis measures, explaining that policy had been "blown off course." In his subsequent postmortem, Brunner diagnosed the weakness as a "yearning for certainty which must always prove chimerical." If the future could be foreseen with certainty it could be planned with confidence.

Political decisions based on guesswork or wrong assumptions are legion. Foreign aid, welfare, subsidized rents, fair wage laws, all have worthy objectives, but so long as the underlying principles are not understood the objectives are not achieved. Worse still, when results turn out badly, blame is put on a failure to apply the legislation correctly or with sufficient vigor. In such cases, more of the same "remedies" result only in surer deterioration in the economy. That is why we need to start from the root causes of economic failure.

The failure of politicians

Many politicians and commentators believe there can be little variation between the policies of government and opposition. Since things are the way they are, and since vast sums of money are required to continue policies which are already decided and which cannot easily be changed, the policies pursued by the two parties cannot be very different. Two classic examples are Labor's continuance of Conservative mistakes in atomic energy after 1964 and the Conservative persistence with Labor's Concorde aircraft program after 1970.

People will tend to vote for the opposition party once the other has been in power long enough to demonstrate that it cannot correct the situation, or produce the desired result. In this sense party voting is negative. One may legitimately ask: "Is anyone in charge?" or "Must the boat go over the rapids?" There may be slight variations in the alternative policies put forward to avoid disaster, but the choice the voter has is very slim.

One self-imposed limitation of politicians is that they are very busy and have little, if any, time for research. MPs have an impossible job when government becomes involved in every detail of our lives. Laws reach the statute book without proper discussion. This result is inevitable so long as parliament is trying to do work which no parliament can ever do.

The average politician does little or no research, but without a sound understanding of principles he is unlikely to be constructive. It is easy to be negative and easiest of all for a politician in opposition to be critical when the ruling party has been in government long enough to have proved itself no better than the last. This is why politicians spend much time attacking each other and the public gets bored with the process. Mr. Enoch Powell is one of the exceptions to the rule that politicians seldom do research. He does make reasoned speeches based on research which in consequence achieve wide publicity and have won him many followers.

Research publications issued by a political party are bound to be biased, and therefore attract little attention from the press and the intellectual world. The many political compromises in producing a "package deal" will probably mean that the policy cannot resist increasing taxation and government action, thereby helping to build up the syndrome which is so harmful. Because government decision-making is not based on principles, an inevitable result is that countless "deals" are made to meet the demands of pressure groups. As each group seeks to achieve privileges at the expense of others, and as all the others are doing exactly the same, the ultimate result must be a highly uneconomic system based on restraint and compulsion. Lacking fundamental principles as guides, the politician and his party organization are like amateur explorers marching in step to an unknown destination without a map, navigational equipment, or any real knowledge of the stars.

The impact of ideas

Almost as though he were predicting the influence of his own ideas since the war, Lord Keynes wrote:

> . . . the ideas of economists and political philosophers, both when they are right and when they are wrong, are more powerful than is commonly understood. Indeed the world is ruled by little else. Practical men, who believe themselves to be quite exempt from any intellectual influences, are usually the slaves of some defunct economist . . . soon or late, it is ideas, not vested interests, which are dangerous for good or evil.[1]

Those whom Keynes saw as wielding influence are the intellectuals who pick up new ideas (or forgotten old ideas) and propagate them in the press, radio, television, and books. These are the journalists, script-writers, academics, authors, and other "experts."

The politician is apt to be an avid reader of the press. He wishes to gauge public opinion as a way of winning or holding on to power, prestige, and votes. Yet so long as he hopes to become a leader by being a follower, he must eventually fail. To be a leader requires an understanding of fundamental ideas and how to put them into practice, probably running counter to current fashions, as the wide following of Mr. Powell may perhaps prove to some even who do not always agree with him.

The quotation from Keynes implies that backroom research can be effective "for good or evil," and the undoubted influence of Adam Smith and Karl Marx provides contrasting examples of this process. The success of new ideas depends on at least one person not only understanding the case, but also writing it down for others to study. If the report is convincing and has a good summary, and even a summary of a summary, it will be read, reviewed and increasingly taught to others. In due time, it will produce consequences.

Perhaps the most obvious of all political mistakes is the belief that it is possible to make the poor richer by taking from the rich.

> The redistribution of incomes has this remarkable feature, that the majority of both its champions and its opponents believe that it happens in a sense that it does not. . . . The reason is that though our system does indeed tax the rich exceptionally heavily, the magnitude of the total effect is misconceived. There simply are not enough rich to make much difference. . . . The modern high-taxing, high-spending state does not obtain its vast revenues from the rich but from heavy taxes on all citizens, including the poor.[2]

The evidence reviewed later indicates that such policies will cause confusion and may benefit the poor only briefly, if at all. It is, on the other hand, possible to establish an economy in which the choices of the poor are maximized, and it is the principles which produce this consequence that are not understood. Having decided our objectives, we must work out the principles which will produce the desired outcome and then write the result down clearly, as I try to do in Chapter 6.

What is "politically impossible"?

If Socrates was right in saying that no one does wrong on purpose, then differences about what is right are probably due more to lack of understanding than to villainy. Thus it is confusion over such words as "aid," "welfare," "subsidy" that has led both political parties in Britain astray. Any discussion about radically alternative policies invariably produces the reply that it is "politically impossible."

For example, from the inception of the British Egg Marketing

Board in 1957 until its demise in 1968, I was one of very few who tried to point out that the subsidy was leading to harmful consequences for the very producers it was intended to help. I was constantly told that I must compromise and conform, and that since it was "politically impossible" to get rid of the board and the subsidy, we had to learn to live with them. I persevered in making speeches and circulating memoranda until by 1967 the consequences of the board and the subsidy were so painful that it suddenly became "politically possible" to get rid of both. Thus the case had been documented and was ready to influence events as soon as circumstances made people think again.

Among policies which were once thought "politically impossible" in Britain we may recall the introduction of commercial television (1955), the abolition of resale price maintenance (1964), legislation on trade unions (1971), floating exchange rates (1972), freeing the price of gold (1972), phasing out rent subsidies (1973). All were documented long before the changes came about. Policies still thought "politically impossible" which will equally certainly be introduced as the case is more fully documented and better understood include the replacement of public monopoly welfare services (especially medical care and education) by private competing suppliers, loans in place of grants for university students (and other categories), denationalization of state industries, and the drastic reduction of government spending and taxation.

An explosive example

It may be difficult to win attention for a most convincing case for radical reform unless it is written down. When in 1940 Dr. (later Sir) Barnes Wallis wanted government support for his large bomb to destroy the Mohne Dam, which supplied power and water for the Ruhr industries,[3] he went to see Lord Beaverbrook and explained the technique he proposed. "You know how short we are of staff," said Beaverbrook, "this thing's *only a theory*. We'd have to stop work on other projects to make it, and then it might be a flop."

Here was a classic example of the businessman's natural skepticism of academics and theories. Wallis had a keen ally in Sir Arthur (later Lord) Tedder, chief of research and development at the Air Ministry; but after he left for the Middle East Wallis was told that the Air Council seemed wary of big bombs. Indeed, the verdict was that anyone who thought of ten-ton bombs was mad. Wallis decided to write a treatise on his bomb, explaining each step so lucidly that a layman could follow it. The resulting book was then sent to seventy influential men in science, politics, and the RAF.

The first result was a visit from a secret serviceman who reprimanded Wallis for sending through the post what had apparently become "vital and very secret." Shortly afterwards, Sir Henry Tizard, scientific adviser to the Ministry of Aircraft Production, felt moved to form a committee to study the proposal. The consequences we all know. The bomb was built and the raid was successful.

Even if it were true that those in authority will not listen and do not want to learn, each worsening spasm in the economy will make more people willing to listen. As taxes rise and controls encroach deeper on individual choice, more ears will be attentive.

Doubters will say, "Even if you are correct in arguing that we must think out the right policy, there is not time; things are so desperate that we must take action now." Since this is tantamount to saying that politicians must act without thinking first, we must turn to history to show how thinking can help.

3
Look Back at History
LEARNING FROM MANY LANDS IN MANY AGES

My study of many episodes in the past has convinced me that man's decision-making can and does govern events. My reading of history suggests that there are principles which can be learned and which can help us achieve certain consequences. And if governments fly in the face of these principles, we can predict the kind of troubles that will follow.

I propose to review some of the extensive historical evidence in the light of my primary principle: when choice is maximized increased prosperity follows. If my basic thinking is correct, we will find that where governments have deliberately reduced individual choice—often with the best possible intentions—the increase in prosperity will be slowed down or even reversed. Sometimes when governments have vigorously pursued a policy of reducing choice, prosperity has vanished into chaos—and on at least one occasion into oblivion.

SOME PAINFUL LESSONS

After 1918, when the American government was unwinding its wartime controls, Mary G. Lacy (librarian of the Department of Agriculture in Washington) was invited to review the history of official efforts to fix prices. The result was a paper entitled "Food Control During Forty-Six Centuries: A Contribution to the History of Price Fixing." She concluded:

> The history of government limitation of price seems to teach one clear lesson: that in attempting to ease the

burdens of the people in a time of high prices by artificially setting a limit on them, the people are not relieved but only exchange one set of ills for another which is greater. Among these ills are the withholding of goods from the market . . . the dividing of the community into two hostile camps, one only of which considers that the government acts in its interests, and the practical difficulties of enforcing such limitation in prices. . . .

Mary Lacy showed that in trying to deal with inflation governments had on many occasions deliberately interfered with individual choice. She summarized numerous examples of government interference which, despite the best intentions for "the good of the people," produced the opposite results of impoverishing them and reducing choice. The Greeks, some 2,500 years ago, coined the word *stasis* to describe such traumatic occasions.

The Roman Empire

The classic example of the attempt by government to improve the lot of the people by restricting their choice is that of the Emperor Diocletian about the year AD 300. He was faced with the familiar problem of rising prices in the wake of an increase in the quantity of money and a debasement in its value. As the historian Duruy tells us:

Under the impression that to give to a piece of metal whatever value they liked, it sufficed to engrave the Emperor's name upon it, the Roman Government had ended by putting in circulation pieces of "silver" and "gold" which contained neither silver nor gold. . . . Very high prices resulted therefore from the depreciation of the currency.[1]

The modern reader will not, therefore, be surprised to know that in the preface to his famous Edict of AD 301, Diocletian declared:

All men know that articles of traffic and objects of daily use have attained exorbitant prices, four or eight times their true value, or even more than that; so that, through the avarice of monopolies, the provisioning of our armies becomes impossible.

Miss Lacy quotes the historian Abbott as follows:

In his effort to bring prices down to what he considered a normal level, Diocletian did not content himself with such half measures as we are trying in our attempts to suppress combinations in restraint of trade, but he boldly fixed the maximum prices at which beef, grain, eggs, clothing, and other articles should be sold, and prescribed the penalty of death for anyone who disposed of his wares at a higher figure.[2]

By today's standards, Diocletian's task was relatively simple. We are told that he had to fix prices for no more than between 700 and 800 items, which were all that were commonly traded in those days, along with the wages of teachers, advocates, bricklayers, tailors, weavers, physicians, and humbler callings.

The modern reader will hardly be surprised to hear that the result of such coercive efforts to dictate artificial prices for goods and services was total failure. In the more dramatic words of Lactantius, a contemporary historian writing within a decade or so of the event, the considered verdict on Diocletian was as follows:

After many oppressions which he put in practice had brought a general dearth upon the empire, he set himself to regulate the prices of all vendible things. There was also much blood shed upon very slight and trifling accounts; and the people brought provisions no more to markets, since they could not get a reasonable price for them; and this increased the dearth so much, that at last after many had died by it, the law itself was laid aside.[3]

One brighter note to emerge from Miss Lacy's catalogue of repeated error was that Diocletian had better success in his subsequent effort with the alternative policy of currency reform, which might be regarded as the ancient equivalent of monetary policy—to which I believe present-day governments will yet have to return before inflation is tackled at its monetary source. Even so, it was left to Emperor Constantine to restore confidence and stability by re-introducing a reliable currency based on gold which the people knew could not be debased for the convenience of politicians—as could paper or other substitute currencies.

On such efforts to restrict choice by controlling prices, in a vain effort to combat the fall in value of a debased currency, another Roman historian, M. Rostovtzeff, wrote:

> The same expedient had often been tried before him and was often tried after him. As a temporary measure in a critical time, it might be of some use. As a general measure intended to last, it was certain to do great harm and to cause terrible bloodshed, without bringing any relief. Diocletian shared the pernicious belief of the ancient world in the omnipotence of the state, a belief which many modern theorists continue to share with him and with it.[4]

Usury in England

If "choice maximized" means the most rapid increase in prosperity, any restriction of it should be viewed with suspicion. Yet in the eighth century Christians were forbidden to lend or borrow money by charging or paying interest. Since this ecclesiastical law did not prevent people wishing to borrow, it is not surprising that the Jews, who had no foolish inhibitions about payment, became bankers and money lenders.

In 1364 Edward III empowered the City of London to issue an ordinance against usury and an act of Parliament with a similar objective was passed in 1390. As one might suppose, those who wished to lend or borrow found many loopholes in the law which resulted in the more stringent Act of 1487, which proved equally vain and was repealed in 1495. Henry VIII legalized the lending of money at interest up to 10 per cent in 1545. In 1552 another attempt was made to prohibit usury, but when it failed Queen Elizabeth legalized the lending of money at interest with the limit still at 10 per cent. In 1624 this limit was reduced to 8 per cent and in 1651 to 6 per cent. From then on the argument over the legality of charging interest concentrated merely on the rate, until the restrictions were removed altogether in 1854. What is certain is that if an artificially low rate of interest had been successfully enforced in the 19th century, capital investment would have been held back and the growth in standards of living retarded.

Wat Tyler

Every British schoolboy knows, or used to know, about Wat Tyler and his rebellion of 1381, but probably few appreciate that it arose from an attempt by the British government to freeze wages.

Sir Arthur Bryant[5] tells how Black Death or bubonic plague reduced the population by about half in twenty-five years. The resulting labor shortage naturally led to a spectacular rise in wages, which parliaments, controlled by landowners, tried to prevent by punitive ordinances and legislation. In these days of increasing strike action, it is interesting to read:

> In the thirty years after the first post-Black Death statute against what Council and parliament called "the *malice* of laborers," nearly nine thousand cases of wage enforcement were tried by the courts and in nearly all judgment was given in the employer's favor. [My emphasis.]

Not surprisingly, Sir Arthur tells us: "These Statutes of Laborers aroused bitter class-feeling." Despite repressive legislation we read of evasion by

> . . . surly villeins standing idle in the fields or trampling in angry companies to the nearest town to sell their labor to those who would pay highest for it.

The pilgrims in New England

The coming of the pilgrims to the New England coast in 1620

marked the first "socialist" experiment in America. It failed within three years when the settlers discovered that, for their very survival, they had to turn to what we now know as the free market system because minimized choice did not work. We can still learn a valuable lesson from this early failure of socialism, which I believe is best described as a system of minimized individual choice.

Before landing, the pilgrims entered into what is known as the Mayflower Compact, under which Plymouth was set up as a share-the-wealth community. Nobody owned anything and whatever was produced became common property. They lived under this system from the desperate first winter of 1620-21 until the hungry spring of 1623, when they changed to a market system. The reason was explained by William Bradford (one of the leading original pilgrims and second governor of Plymouth Colony) in a tract entitled *Of Plimoth Plantation*. He describes how common ownership

> . . . was found to breed much confusion and discontent and ritard imployment that would have been to their benefits and comforte. For the young men that were most able and fitte for labor and service did repine that they should spend their time and strength to worke for other mens wives and children, without any recompense. The strong . . . had no more in devision of victails and cloaths than he that was weake . . . Upon the poynte all being to have alike, and all to doe alike, they thought themselves in the like condition, and one as good as another. And so, if it did not cut off those relations that God hath set amongst men, yet it did at least much diminish and take of the mutuall respects that should be preserved amongst them.

Instead of a Thanksgiving feast in the fall of 1622, there were starvation and a collapse of morale.

> So they begane to thinke how they might raise as much corne as they could . . . that they might not still thus

languish in misere. At last, after much debate of things, the governor gave way that they should set corne every man for his own particular. . . . And so assigned to every family a parcell of land. . . . This had very good success for it made all hands very industrious, so as much more corne was planted than other waise would have bene.

The Thanksgiving feast in the fall of 1623 was, in plain truth, a celebration of their deliverance from socialism. Bradford philosophized:

The experience that was had in this commone course and condition, tried sundrie years, and that amongst Godly and sober men, may well evince the Vanitie of that conceite of Plato's and other ancients, applauded by some of later times, that the taking away of propertie and bringing in communitie into a commone wealth would make them happy and flourishing; as if they were wiser than God.

It was this freeing of individual choice for consumers no less than producers that prepared the way for the miracle of American economic development.

I would certainly claim the constitution of 1787 as a further step which helped to maximize choice in the U. S.A. Its provisions were thought out with great care and reflected the accumulated wisdom of the time. It was the child of much tribulation and conflict, as had been our own Magna Carta. The constitution was based on the sanctity of the individual and the protection of private property. Once again, it was an attempt to maximize choice by preventing any individual exercising his freedom at the expense of others. Again, we find that the nation that has applied these principles in government prospers. Is this chance, or is there a definite cause-and-effect relationship?

For 150 years after the constitution, the U.S. economy prospered. Maximized choice resulted in more and more voluntary exchanges and stimulated an unprecedented increase in wealth. It is no coincidence that this miracle has faltered in recent years as

American governments have exerted increasing powers of taxation and control over industry and trade.

Competitive mail services

The postal services have always been considered a natural government monopoly. What is surprising is the number of occasions individuals have challenged this monopoly and produced a better service.[6]

The originator of the first penny post was William Dockwra in 1680. He introduced the world's first stamp, a hand-struck triangular design bearing the words "Penny Post Paid." He provided insurance on anything up to £12 at no extra charge and established the first house-to-house delivery service with ten deliveries a day. He was so successful that the Duke of York, who operated the government Post Office service in London, sued him for infringing the state monopoly. It took two years to shut down Dockwra and he was fined £100 for contempt. The state took over his collecting stations and converted most of them into branches of the GPO.

In 1709 another adventurer, Charles Povey, set up a halfpenny carriage, with postmen who called to collect as well as deliver. Penny posts began to spring up everywhere and by 1800 over 2,000 of them had been established in the British Isles. A man named Williamson set up a penny post in Scotland and it was seventeen years before the GPO took him over when, instead of being fined, he was awarded a pension.

In his book *Men Against the State*,[7] James J. Martin reports that in the U.S.A.,

> From 1841 to 1845, steady inroads on the revenues of the federal post office department were made by private enterprise companies. It was a source of embarrassment to the Democratic administration of the period to see mail companies making profits from carrying letters for 5 and 10 cents each, while providing a service somewhat more expeditious than that furnished by the federal postal system.

Here was competition acting highly efficiently as "a discovery procedure." The predictable government response was a bill whose sponsor frankly explained

> that there was to be no attempt at competing with these firms; they were to be put out of business by "penal enactment."

Time and again we see that people in government prefer to use their power to prevent choice and competition rather than to direct their efforts to improving their services and leaving customers with freedom to go elsewhere.

Encore in France

In a society where choice is maximized, each individual exercises power by his decisions to buy or sell on terms he chooses. Such freedom enables him to protect himself against bad government or other oppressive monopoly power. One such choice, which incompetent governments periodically try to take away from their citizens, is the ability to buy and sell gold. Many say that gold has no value except in the manufacture of ornaments, plate, and jewelry. But, as we shall see, any product (or money) has a value that can be truly assessed only by the readiness of others to offer their goods and services in exchange.

In his introduction to a study of inflation in France,[8] the American writer Henry Hazlitt recalls that in 1789 the minister of finance, Necker, fought for financial rectitude in the hope of keeping France faithful to sound monetary principles. Mr. Dickson White says of Necker:

> Anyone today reading his prophecies of the evils sure to follow such a [paper] currency would certainly ascribe to him a miraculous foresight, were it not so clear that his prophetic power was due simply to a knowledge of natural laws revealed by history.

All the age-old arguments in favor of the creation of money were brought forward, but some still remembered an earlier experience of 1716 when John Law persuaded the French Regent that he could restore French industry from the depression caused by the extravagance and corruption of Louis XIV by starting a bank to issue notes. The bank's notes soon went to a premium, Law having publicly declared at the outset that any banker deserved death who issued notes without sufficient security to answer all demands. Alas, both he and the Regent soon forgot this wise maxim and their initial success led them to think that a paper currency which could supplement gold and silver coin might entirely supersede it.

The bank was so successful that it was granted a monopoly of tobacco and the sole right of refining gold and silver. It effectively became the royal bank of France and promptly issued new notes to the amount of 1,000,000,000 livres. This departure from sound principles was quickly followed by the familiar symptoms of inflation. Bread, meat, and vegetables rose to record prices and the wages of labor climbed in proportion. By 1720 the government felt driven by popular outcry to suspend the convertibility of notes into gold and then to forbid the holding of gold or even the buying of jewelry, plate, and precious stones.

Yet despite these experiences, revolutionary France in 1790 behaved as if it were deliberately staging an encore: the government once again embarked irretrievably on an inflationary process by new issues of paper money. At first a new issue was made of 400,000,000 livres based on the security of the confiscated property of the church, which was supposed to guarantee that the notes would "soon be considered better than the coin now hoarded and will bring it out again into circulation." Mirabeau even proposed to repay the public debts by the issue of 2,400,000,000 livres in legal tender notes and to forbid the use of specie in purchasing national lands. Once again the predictable result followed: prices rose and gold began to disappear from circulation. The blame was variously put on brokers, the Bourbon family, speculators, and foreign merchants, but never on the real culprit, the government itself.

When in the early 1790s the appalling inflation caused the government to run out of foreign money, it resorted to a most fantastic auction of the contents of the palace of Versailles, lasting three hundred and fifty-one days. But selling assets can stave off bankruptcy only for a short time. Meanwhile, Dickson White reports:

> Enterprise received a mortal blow. . . . This state of things, too, while it bore heavily upon the monied classes was still more ruinous to those in moderate, and most of all to those in stricken, circumstances. . . . These evils though great were small compared to those far more deep-seated signs of disease which now showed themselves throughout the country.

Thrift gave way to gambling and extravagance among the rich, while the washerwomen of Paris responded to the high soap price by demanding that the merchants who sold it should be punished by death. Marat thereupon suggested that the people might help themselves literally by hanging shopkeepers and plundering their stores.

In 1793 came the first real price and wage controls, Robespierre's law of the maximum. When it did not work, and goods disappeared from the markets, the guillotine was worked overtime in a vain attempt to enforce the law. Punishment for selling paper assignats against gold or silver at less than their face value was twenty years' imprisonment in chains. Investment in foreign countries carried the death penalty.

Nevertheless, no government decree could prevent the louis d'or from recording the decline in the value of assignats. The gold louis, originally equivalent to 25 francs, was worth about 1,000 paper francs in September 1793 and over 7,000 six months later.

Dickson White's conclusion confirmed the findings of Mary Lacy in 1922 and of Professor Milton Friedman more recently.

> To cure a disease temporary in its character, a corrosive poison was administered, which ate out. the vitals of French prosperity. . . . It ended in the complete financial, moral and political prostration of France.

One Frenchman who learned the correct lesson was Napoleon. When he was hard pressed financially and it was proposed to resort to paper money, he wrote to his minister, "While I live, I will never resort to irredeemable paper." Dickson White comments:

> He never did, and France, under his determination, commanded all the gold she needed. When Waterloo came, with the invasion of the Allies, with war on her own soil, with a change of dynasty, and with heavy expenses for war and indemnities, France on a specie basis experienced no severe financial distress.

Hunger and history

Parmalee Prentice, a son-in-law of the first Rockefeller, in 1951 published a study[9] which described the dismal quality and quantity of foods available to the human race until the establishment of the Enclosure Acts in England at the end of the 18th century. These acts may appear to have restricted choice by combining individual strips of land into larger holdings. In practice they had the opposite effect by protecting private property and enabling farmers to choose for themselves what land, crops, and livestock to cultivate.

Communal farming had previously prevented a good farmer from segregating his cattle from the animals of the bad farmers, while under the open field system crops could be grown only in rotation governed by age-old custom and weeds spread from the neglectful farmer to his neighbor's plots. The Enclosure Acts, by protecting private property and encouraging competition, set in motion forces which rapidly increased farming productivity. It was the resulting agricultural revolution which prepared the way for Britain's industrial revolution. If only the Indian government would learn this lesson it would do more to prevent hunger than by begging any amount of foreign aid to subsidize industrial development.

The great German inflation

An American economist, Hans F. Sennholz, has shown[10] that the disastrous inflation in Germany after the First World War was remarkably like the French experience of the 1790s.

> Immediately after the war, the German government, under the leadership of the Socialist party, embarked upon heavy expenditures for health, education, and welfare. This added to the already heavy load on the treasury for demobilization expenses, the demands by the Armistice. . . . While government expenditures rose by leaps and bounds, the revenue suffered a gradual decline; in October 1923, only 0.8 per cent of government expenses were covered by tax revenues. . . . The depreciation of the currency brought about the destruction of taxable wealth in the form of mortgages and bonds . . . .

Once again the blame was put on the balance of payments, speculators, and ultimately Jews. Professor Sennholz concludes with a prophecy:

> The specious argument that denies the presence of any inflation in terms of purchasing power or gold value may be expected to emerge in later phases of inflation when monetary authorities will desperately seek any argument that promises to hold them blameless.

It was a Conservative minister in Britain who recently joined the chorus blaming "property speculators" for the record inflation since 1972.

The Great Crash

The same author has written[11] about the great slump of the early 1930s which he compares with the business cycles that have plagued the American economy since 1820.

> In each case, government had generated a boom through easy money and credit, which was soon followed by the

inevitable bust. . . . The spectacular crash of 1929 followed five years of reckless credit expansion by the Federal Reserve System under the Coolidge Administration.

To meet a decline in business in 1924, the Reserve Bank suddenly created some $500 million of new money which led inevitably to a bank credit expansion of over $4,000 million in less than one year. The immediate effect was a temporarily agreeable economic boom. Predictably, when the threat of inflation loomed up, the authorities provoked the worst world slump ever by equally suddenly reducing the supply of money and raising protective tariffs, which invited retaliation from other countries and all but throttled international trade. Even such a classic case of government folly, however, has not prevented the legend that the world slump was caused by the failure of the free market!

In an effort to teach the correct lesson from this bit of history, Professor Friedman[12] has renamed the Great Depression the "great contraction," thereby underlining the responsibility of the monetary authorities for their boom-and-bust excesses.

Another crash

Another method used by governments to reduce choice is to nationalize a particular activity and to inhibit competition from private companies. An interesting and little-known test of public enterprise was provided by the Labor Government in 1930. Two large airships were built, one by the state and one by a private firm. One was finished long before the other and crossed the Atlantic and back; while the other on its maiden flight crashed in flames, killing all but six on board. There are no prizes for guessing which of the two was built by the state!

James Leasor in his story of this drama[13] tells how again and again during the building of the state airship wrong business decisions and even wrong technical decisions were made and covered up for political reasons. Compared with the privately built R. 100, which successfully flew to Canada and back and altogether covered more than 20,000 miles with only normal wear and tear, the state-built R.101 cost twice as much and crashed on its maiden flight to India after just managing to get across the channel to France.

The detailed case-study shows up the error of describing such heavy-footed state operations as "public enterprises" when they neither benefit the public nor display true enterprise. There is some evidence that the R.101 crashed because it was overloaded, especially with the air minister's luggage which appears to have increased the maximum payload by *50 per cent* because he was privileged to exceed the limit of ten pounds imposed on everyone else. In this case, we may cite the tragedy as an example of politicians defying economic law and the law of gravity at one and the same time!

The story of two railroads

Professor Howard Stephenson, formerly of Boston University, presented another case study[14] of public and private enterprise in the form of a comparison between two Canadian railroads, the privately-run Canadian Pacific and the nationalized Canadian National. Both had many ancillary activities in road and water transport, but competition was not entirely fair as exemplified by advantages the state conceded to its railroad in air transport.

The comparison of financial results over eighteen years, from 1941 to 1958, revealed that where one company earned a profit of $669 million the other suffered a loss of $663 million. Again, there is no prize for guessing which was the result of nationalization. But it might surprise some readers to hear that in addition to paying its shareholders almost $370 million, the private enterprise company also paid a similar sum in taxation, in contrast to the nationalized company's charge of over $660 million against taxation. No wonder politicians find competition an uncomfortable discovery procedure.

SOME SUCCESS STORIES

I now want to turn to examples where man has not only learnt the right lessons from history but has managed to reverse the syndrome of failure by maximizing rather than minimizing choice. In each case there had been economic confusion or worse until the government deliberately attempted to increase choice, whereupon there was a striking increase in prosperity.

Urukagina of Lagash

The Sumerian civilization, which began to flourish perhaps 6,000 years ago, fortunately developed writing on clay tablets. Some of these have survived sufficiently well to be deciphered recently.

Professor S. N. Kramer has written two excellent books[15] on Sumer which include researches into social reform and taxation. One of the most instructive fragments is the story of Urukagina of Lagash who ruled from about 2,350 BC. Previously a pervasive, obnoxious bureaucracy consisting of the ruler and his palace coterie had perfected the most sinister acts of tyranny and oppression. In the record of Urukagina's sweeping reforms, Professor Kramer tells us that "we find the word 'freedom' used for the first time in man's recorded history." What went before was the familiar sequence of high taxation, confiscation of property, and every conceivable infringement of personal rights and individual choice. A contemporary chronicler recorded that

> The rich, the big men, and the supervisors were getting richer and richer, at the expense of the less fortunate citizens, while from one end of the land to the other there were the tax collectors.

What Urukagina did to correct this sorry state was to switch from a situation where choice was minimized, both because the law no longer protected the individual and because taxes were very high, to a policy which maximized choice. He established a rule of law that protected the rights of individuals, however humble, and prevented the abuse of power, however elevated. One significant legal innovation was his insistence that the Sumerian courts must "make manifest to all, by means of the written word, the guilt for which the accused was punished."

Urukagina swept away the oppressive bureaucracy, established honest weights and measures, including no doubt a reformed currency. The last word must be left to a contemporary historian:

> From one end of the land to the other . . . there were no tax collectors.

It seems to me that enough can be gleaned from this episode to illustrate the contrast between minimized choice, which I equate with tyranny and stagnation, and maximized choice, which is more generally described as freedom and associated with prosperity.

Bengal: 1770 v. 1866

For a brief example of a lesson learnt from history, I can do no better than draw on Hunter's *Annals of Rural Bengal* from Mary Lacy's report.[16]

In 1770 Lower Bengal's rice harvest failed utterly, and fully a third of the population died. The government's response was to prohibit what it was pleased to term the monopoly of grain, thereby preventing prices from rising at once to their natural rates. Left to itself, Hunter argued,

> private enterprise would have stored up the general supply
> at the harvest with a view to realizing a larger profit at a
> later period in the scarcity.

In a free market prices would of course have risen, with the effect of compelling the population to reduce their consumption from the beginning and economize supplies. In this way the pressure of scarcity would be spread over the period to the next harvest, instead of being concentrated in the final months. As Mary Lacy pointed out, by prohibiting all speculation in rice, the government "acted about as sagely as the skipper of a wrecked vessel who should refuse to put his crew upon half rations." The predictable result of the government's well-meaning intervention was to intensify the impact of famine instead of alleviating it.

A century later the government of Bengal faced the famine of 1866 with a very different policy. Far from trying to check speculation, the government facilitated it by publishing weekly returns of prices in every district. As a result, the twin forces of choice and competition worked to bring about the transport of rice from areas of relative abundance to places of worst scarcity. Mary Lacy summarizes the contrasting results which tell their own tale:

In 1770 the price of grain, in place of promptly rising to three half-pence a pound as in 1865-66, continued at three farthings during the earlier months of the famine. During the latter months it advanced to twopence, and in certain localities reached fourpence.

Thus, by refraining from curbs on consumer choice the government averted a repetition of the earlier national disaster.

Free trade–1846

Although understanding is essential before correct policies can be introduced, reform is often helped along by the influence of particular individuals and of favorable circumstances. The German economic miracle was one example of this combination and the repeal of the Corn Laws in Britain almost exactly one hundred years earlier provided another.

The Corn Laws in 1815 prohibited (and in 1828 regulated) the import of wheat and other cereals into Britain unless the home price was high. The aim was to protect both the landed interest and national defense after the Napoleonic Wars had shown the danger of depending on food imports in time of war. On the other hand, there were already thinkers and politicians who followed the teachings of Adam Smith in believing that free trade would be best to promote economic efficiency and, therefore, national strength in peace and war.

From 1820 the Manchester Chamber of Commerce called again and again for free trade which would reduce the price of food and so enable the textile industry and other leaders of the industrial revolution to export more cheaply and advance the general prosperity of the country. Yet in spite of the efforts of Cobden, Bright, and the Cheap Food League, when C. P. Villiers moved a motion in the House of Commons every year to repeal the Corn Laws it was regularly rejected by very large majorities, even in the early 1840s.

Although the idea was increasingly understood, it was not until the failure of the potato crop in 1845 that British ports were thrown open to alternative supplies of food. Thereupon Robert Peel, as Conservative Prime Minister and defender of the agricultural interest, did what up to the last minute in 1846 was thought "politically impossible." He repealed the Corn Laws and thereby made possible half a century of prosperity based upon free trade which did more than anything else to reduce poverty by enlarging the choices open to the poor both in earning and in spending their rising incomes.[17]

The great increase in England's wealth cannot be ascribed to coal which had been there for millennia, nor to particular inventions which in many cases had first been made centuries earlier. My case is that the rapid exploitation of natural resources and human ingenuity was galvanized by the profit mechanism which, in turn, arose from the discovery procedure of competition and free markets. It was only as individuals were free to supply the demands (or choices) of other individuals, on a voluntary basis, that increments of wealth added up to a massive growth in wealth and standards of living.

A Swedish lesson

The history of Sweden between 1860 and 1913 offers another example of apparent prosperity, closely following a recognizable policy for the maximization of individual choice. This example particularly illustrates how changes in legislation can come about because of the effort of an individual thinker working in a back room.

Dr. F. A. Harper[18] has analyzed this period and written:

If we measure economic progress by the rise in output per hour of work, the golden age of Sweden was a period from the early 1860s to the outbreak of World War I. . . . For that period as a whole, Sweden's average rate of increase was 2.76 per cent yearly, compounded. This far exceeds any level of increase in the United States for a sustained period of time.

Economic progress in Sweden since 1913, though quite irregular, has been at a rate about one-third less than for the prior half-century . . . wages left for the Swedish earner to spend on objects of his own choice were cut sharply by increasing taxes over the last half century.

Sweden, like most other European nations before about 1860, was strongly mercantilist and tried all sorts of controls in a vain effort to achieve higher living standards. The definite economic change both internally and externally in the early 1860s was, according to Harper, the result of the influence of the works of J.B. Say and later of the powerful influence of Frederic Bastiat, the noted French liberal.

Harper records that Bastiat's influence came to Sweden in the following way:

A Swedish gentleman by the name of John August Gripenstedt, on one of his visits to France, made the acquaintance of Bastiat and established a friendship founded on deep admiration. Gripenstedt became a top political leader in Sweden using lines of reasoning quite clearly identified with Bastiat in his political speeches.

By 1860, Harper tells us, Gripenstedt managed to:

. . . do away with all prohibitions against imports or exports, to abolish all export duties, to reduce the import tariffs for manufactured goods and to establish free trade in agricultural products . . . Sweden's golden age of half a century followed.

The German economic miracle

We now come to the most fascinating example of all. In 1948 Germany was in a state of economic collapse. Inflation paralyzed industry and business. Postwar reconstruction was at a standstill and morale could hardly have been lower. Suddenly, Dr. Ludwig Erhard, the minister of economic affairs, introduced a new policy based on choice and competition with a result that has been called the Economic Miracle.

At the end of the Second World War, Germany had been reduced to the physical level of an underdeveloped country, as films taken at the time demonstrate. The population of the western portion, about half of the Germany of 1939, was 13 per cent larger by the addition of some twelve million refugees. Although by 1947 other European countries were recovering rapidly from the war, the situation in Germany remained abysmal.[19] By 1948, industrial production was still only half the 1936 level. Exports were one-tenth and imports one-quarter the level in 1938. Infant mortality was high and food consumption low. The devastation was such that only those who had seen it could believe it.[20] I remember lunching with a German family near Cologne in 1947: the meal consisted of some cooked vegetables and the luxury, kept to the end, was a small piece of white bread.

Before the 1948 currency reform, the German economy was blanketed by a network of controls, especially price and wage controls intended to offset the effects of the substantial monetary expansion of the war. At artificially low prices, however, goods failed to move except via black markets. In Erhard's words, the economy "had returned to a state of primitive barter."[21]

Economic observers expected that Germany would be permanently weakened economically. Indeed, in the immediate postwar years policy-makers made it a definite objective of policy to reduce the country to a permanently rural state. The Morgenthau Plan envisaged that ten million workers would be shifted from industry into agriculture,[22] while the Potsdam Declaration advocated the restriction of German industrial output to a level of some

45 per cent below that of 1936. The later Anglo-American Industrial Plan of 1946 would have permitted the level of output to equal that of 1936, although the population was larger.

It was against this bleak background that Dr. Erhard introduced his radical economic reforms of July 1948. They replaced the inflated Reichsmarks with a smaller supply of Deutschemarks and threw "into the wastepaper basket, at one swoop, hundreds of decrees, promulgating controls. . . ."[23] The immediate impact of this release of market forces was striking:

> The black market suddenly disappeared. Shop windows were full of goods, factory chimneys were smoking, and the streets swarmed with lorries. Everywhere the noise of new buildings going up replaced the deathly silence of the ruins. If the state of recovery was a surprise, its swiftness was even more so.
>
> In all sectors of economic life, it began as the clock struck on the day of currency reform. Shops filled up with goods from one day to the next; the factories began to work. On the eve of currency reform the Germans were aimlessly wandering about their towns in search of a few additional items of food. A day later they thought of nothing but producing them. One day apathy was mirrored on their faces, while on the next the whole nation looked hopefully into the future.[24]

There was, however, much opposition to the new policy. For the British Labor ministers, busy applying their favorite policies of controls, one can only imagine their consternation at Erhard's action. In Germany, the trade unions called for a general strike and the civil service began secretly drafting new decrees for the re-establishment of controls.

The attitude of socialist economists was revealingly illustrated by the severe attack from Dr. Thomas (now Lord) Balogh.[25] Within two years of the great experiment in freedom, he denounced the currency reform and its supporting program for monetary stability as "savage deflation." This policy, he said,

. . . beggared the middle classes and the workers, just as they had been robbed by the great inflation of the First War. The instability of the German social system has irredeemably been intensified. The eventual political consequences cannot be estimated.

The superiority of the pre-Erhard régime of direct controls was emphasized.

Control over production and consumption represents the most effective and flexible means of imposing relative pressures, equivalent to localized deflation, on industry without incurring the need for a general cut in income, causing unnecessary hardship and unemployment. . . . By direct controls, demand can be cut to fit in with productive or export/import bottlenecks and the resulting excess demand directed to innocuous uses. . . .

Finally, Balogh predicted the failure of the whole scheme:

The German Government tried to apply to real-life an abstract, obsolescent and internally inconsistent economic theory. . . . There are two tests of an economic policy—first, does it increase national income? Second, does it distribute the product justly? The German experiment failed in both.

This partisan analysis provides a classic example of a mistaken assessment based on a preference for policies that reduce other people's choice. It is similar to the line of argument used by economists who advocate incomes policy which reduces choice without achieving the aim of solving inflation.

However, by 1956, Balogh was commending the German example to Britain's Conservative Government:

Between 1950 and 1955 [West Germany] invested more than twice as much as Britain[26]. . . . Real wages in England rose only 12.3 per cent since 1950 against 24 per cent in the US and 39 per cent in Germany.[27]

But then even an unsympathetic intellectual would have to acknowledge that it was not quite a "failure" for Germany to more than treble exports and almost double money incomes between 1949 and 1956 while the cost of living rose only 14 per cent.[28] By 1960, Balogh acknowledged that Germany had established itself as "the unchallenged economic leader in Europe,"[29] and went further to admit:

> The fact stands out that in Germany, France, and Japan the improvement in workers' earnings and social benefits was at a rate two or three times as high, despite a worsening of the distribution of income, than in Britain.

It was the classical liberal economist Wilhelm Röpke who drew the true lesson of Erhard's success.[30]

> Now there is much talk about the German miracle. For the economist there is no miracle. It is a very simple story of ending economic paralysis and disorder brought about by planning and inflation and ending it by sound economic order based on two things. First, the freedom of goods and markets, and second on discipline in the field of money . . . the idea was simple. The difficult thing was to put it into practice . . . the miracle was that this return to wisdom and common sense was possible on the political and social levels and at a time in which collectivism and inflationism seemed to be triumphant. This had been the essence of National and Socialist economic policy during the Third Reich.

As one of the intellectual inspirers, along with Professor Walter Eucken, of Erhard's policy, Röpke might be forgiven a parting quip and prophecy.

> It might be almost amusing today to collect all the wrong prophecies and desperate theories which have been invented in order to disprove the striking evidence of the German experiment . . . the Socialists, if they do not want to be defeated in the elections, have to assure that they

believe in the market economy and a sound currency . . .
so economic law has triumphed over Karl Marx.

Although more recently German governments have fallen victims
to some of the wrong policies practiced elsewhere in Europe, for a
time the success of Erhard's reforms was proved by the anxiety of
the German Social Democrats to assure voters that they were no
longer a socialist party.

Understanding the key

From many centuries and diverse countries, I have summarized case histories of circumstances where tribulation has
caused men to pause and think as a necessary preliminary before
acting to maximize choice. The pages of history confirm that on
the few occasions when this has been done the results have been
highly beneficial.

It emerges that apparently isolated individuals in a backroom
can be tremendously effective for both good and ill. Adam Smith,
Karl Marx, Cobden, Röpke, Eucken, and Bastiat are all men of
theory who have produced more far-reaching consequences than
they may dared to have hoped. The consequences have been
achieved not by weight of numbers, but often by the understanding
of individuals. In most cases this understanding had been
documented before it was implemented.

One outstanding instance of the ability and power of one man
is the story of the farmer Gideon, as told in the Book of Judges.
When the Midianites had beaten the Israelites, Gideon, an Israelite
of no great standing, collected 32,000 men for battle to free his
people. Being a Jew he believed in a wise God, to whom he turned
in deep thought and prayer. The guidance he received was as
follows:

> The people that are with thee are too many for me to give
> the Midianites into their hands, lest Israel vaunt them-
> selves against me, saying, Mine own hand hath saved me.

Instead, Gideon was told: ''Tell the people that all who are afraid should return home," and 22,000 went home, leaving 10,000. But God was still not satisfied and required Gideon to select only 300.

Then by the simplest of strategies, with the surprise use of trumpets and lights after dark and without weapons, the Midianites were scared into flight. Without a warlike stroke Gideon was shown how to win a battle. Wisdom, not numbers or force, conquered.

My conclusion from this excursion through the pages of history is that the reduction of individual choice and competition does harm, but that their increase achieves conditions of widening prosperity. Maximum freedom of individual choice in economic decisions can achieve wonders even when there is little or no freedom to vote. Under autocratic Caesar Augustus in the early years of the first century BC, taxes were low, trade was free, and Roman wealth expanded at an exceptional rate.

The prospect of finding a benevolent dictator who will apply legislation designed to free the individual is slender. Despite its shortcomings, the democratic way is our best hope of restoring choice, particularly when ordinary voters are beginning to rebel against the burdens of over-government and over-taxation. But the plain warning of history is that if we do not assert the right to choose for ourselves others will impose their choices on us.

4
Look Around
LEARNING FROM OUR OWN TIMES

To learn lessons from the history of postwar Britain, I turn first to agriculture because most of my practical experience since 1945 has been gained from farming in Sussex. That was where I developed the new industry of broiler chickens in the 1950s and where I still run a modern dairy farm of 400 acres. Furthermore, agriculture is man's oldest occupation and still provides for our basic needs. Why, then, have governments tolerated and even encouraged restrictions on competition and choice which hold back efficient methods that could make food cheaper and farmers more prosperous?

AGRICULTURAL "WELFARE"

Despite man's superior mental abilities, his main energies until recent times have had to be concentrated on producing enough to eat. So long as man has difficulties in feeding himself, he cannot turn to more advanced objectives. In countries developing most rapidly, food production has become very efficient. In this process, employment in farming has fallen which has inevitably led to economic changes that can be uncomfortable for some. Where governments plan to maximize choice, the economy will be flexible so that people will move more easily from forms of production in less demand to those in greater demand, where pay or prospects are better.

But where government claims it can solve such adjustments to change without disturbing people in their existing employments, there will naturally be ever-increasing demands on government. If the economy is not flexible, adaptation will be delayed until it becomes irresistible, and even more painful changes are necessary.

"Protection" from what?

Successive British governments have passed legislation, notably the acts of 1947 and 1954, specifically designed to protect farmers and offer them assured markets. It has been assumed that, without government aid, farmers could not stay in business and the public would not get the food it wants.

Theory confirms the lessons of experience and history that the price mechanism is a fabulous information system, cheaper and more effective even than computers. Inevitably in a world of change, it often transmits messages of changing prices and costs which the individual does not like. No one welcomes being told that his products or services are worth less or are not required: the natural response is to blame someone else or seek protection from unpleasant reality, and seek legislation which tries to shelter the farmer from competition or other changes. When the individual's inability to compete is due to inefficiency or changes in demand, such protection only conceals and intensifies the problem.

It is one thing to want a measure of stability or continuity, but quite another to expect to create conditions in which everyone who chooses can produce whatever he decides and stay in profitable business. Lasting stability can be achieved only by a flexible price system. Who is to know what volume of production or level of prices is in the national interest? Such clichés presuppose an omniscient and omnicompetent government. With the best will in the world no one can discover or decide in advance what it is in the national interest to produce, since the range of possibilities is infinite and changes all the time with new discoveries, techniques, and consumer preferences.

Another favorite cliché is that government should "provide adequate remuneration for those who live by the land." But how can any politician or professor or, least of all, farmers' union decide what is fair remuneration? Some people prefer to live in the country even though they earn less than in town. Some are highly efficient and can expand their businesses. Is this to be prevented? How can perpetual changes in methods and markets be reconciled with guaranteed fair incomes or fixed prices?

As a leading poultry producer in the 1960s, I sat on a committee to advise the minister of agriculture on the likely future course of prices in the industry. Under the then-prevailing prices and incomes policy, it was accepted that poultry was one of the products for which prices would be allowed to vary, and leading producers in their private capacity were invited to help warn the ministry of changes. Such meetings provided minor examples of expensive procedures which waste much time and may do serious harm, especially when they lead businessmen to expect salvation from government instead of taking corrective measures to help themselves.

Thus, on one occasion, an industry representative asked the government to prevent cheap turkeys being imported from Denmark. I found it necessary to point out that, whereas a temporary ban on the importation of a few turkeys or chickens might protect the British price slightly for a short time, other regulations were already raising the costs of poultry farmers. I was referring to the minimum import prices (MIP) established for cereals with the aim of ensuring a "reasonable" price for cereal-growers in the United Kingdom. The effect was that even if grain were available at a lower price, importers were not allowed to buy it at less than the MIP. The result was to leave an extra profit in the pockets of the foreign supplier and to raise the cost of cereals to the poultry producer so that we were paying more foreign exchange than necessary when Britain was supposed to have a balance-of-payments crisis.

The intentions were no doubt good, but they could never be achieved because the method of restricting choice must produce negative consequences. As we shall see, the Common Agricultural Policy in Europe operates on similar lines and can therefore never be anything but a disaster for consumers and in the long run for many farmers.

Take eggs . . .

Successive British governments have attempted to help egg producers in the "obvious" way by penalizing the rich through taxes and market controls and giving the poor a subsidy and protection from competition. Both taxes and controls represent government attempts to improve the lot of someone by reducing individual choice. The British Egg Marketing Board (BEMB), created in 1956, was a classic example of an attempt to produce a compulsory welfare situation for farmers. In 1969 the annual subsidy was £20 million, which might seem a large benefit for producers but in practice the result was quite otherwise. At first the subsidy raised the price received by producers but then the market mechanism began to operate. The inevitable result was to encourage production above the level of consumer demand. Without a rigid system of restriction on output, most subsidies lead to overproduction which ultimately harms the intended beneficiary.

Some years ago I remember attending a National Farmers' Union meeting when a member praised the NFU for achieving an extra penny a gallon for milk at the annual price review. In this farmer's mind there was no awareness that an increase in price might harm farmers by stimulating supply and so leading to lower prices later. This example demonstrates how people fail to grasp that price is both a consequence and a cause. There is no such thing as a just price, any more than there is a just thermometer reading. There are right prices and wrong prices. The right price is the one that balances supply and demand most nearly, thereby bringing stability to the market. Stability requires flexibility, like walking a tightrope with a balancing bar. Interfere or remove the market mechanism and producers lack direction indicators and lose their way. The free market is not perfect and cannot produce complete stability; but it works towards that end in a way no other method can do. Methods which deny individual choice in the market must work towards instability.

Despite large expenditures on advertising, research, and administration, the failure of the BEMB was shown by the increasing, mostly illegal, free trade in eggs, known as farm-gate sales, which brought the producer six old pennies more a dozen than the board's eggs carrying the lion trademark, plus a subsidy then running at sixpence a dozen. The culmination of a decade of well-intentioned intervention and subsidy by the board was thus a remarkable differential between the two shillings and sixpence obtained for lion eggs and three shillings and sixpence for those sold in the free market. Something had to happen and, following an official inquiry which established the relationship between economic cause and effect, the end of both board and subsidy was announced in January 1969 by the minister of agriculture in a socialist government. The "politically impossible" had happened.

Although the board was replaced by a new authority, the subsidy was cut from £20 million to £3 million, which will not be as damaging to the industry as the old system. I certainly thought my years of almost singlehanded opposition to the theory and practice of the BEMB had been well-rewarded.

Although postwar governments have attempted to interfere with the price of most farm products in addition to eggs, chicken meat production escaped because it had not developed on a sufficiently large scale when the laws were made. The result of this happy accident of timing was a rapidly growing industry which by any standards became increasingly efficient, probably the most efficient form of agricultural production, and has converted chicken from an occasional luxury dish to an everyday meal which is cheaper than other meats.

. . . and milk

The Milk Marketing Board (MMB) is more damaging than the Egg Board because it has a more complete monopoly. In the name of "co-operative marketing," government coercion is used to fix identical retail prices throughout the country and virtually identical wholesale prices. Farmers are no longer responsible for transport costs. However remote from their market, they are subsidized through the pooling of costs and receipts. Since 1933 when the board was created, production has grown most rapidly where transport costs are highest. The result is to raise costs and aggravate the problem of surplus milk. By fixing prices too high, a surplus is produced which the board tries to dispose of by a classic example of monopolistic price discrimination.

For example, in 1970 when the board paid all farmers about 40 pence a gallon, it sold what it could to liquid wholesalers (i.e., for drinking as milk) at about 50 pence a gallon. The inevitable surplus went to manufacturers (i.e., for making into cheese, butter, powder, etc.) at about 20 pence a gallon. Even so, manufactured milk products had difficulty in competing with imports from distant New Zealand where summer milk fetched about 14 pence a gallon. For liquid milk the British housewife paid 96 pence a gallon compared with the 40 pence received by farmers.

When the MMB and the National Farmers' Union succeeded in getting import quotas against competition from foreign butter, the result was to switch New Zealand producers to cheese production against which "voluntary" quotas were then raised. Such restrictions provide no lasting remedy. They neither discourage home production nor encourage lower costs of distribution at home. Accordingly, they provoke anguished demands from dairy farmers for domestic quotas to reduce home production and keep prices up. Thus we see how market interference designed to protect farmers simply distorts production and buttresses inefficiency.

Only when the MMB is disbanded will the retail price to housewives fall to a competitive market level. Then, because production will no longer be artificially stimulated by guaranteed prices, the earnings of farmers situated in the right places will rise and more efficient organization should make milk production into a soundly-based growth industry.[1]

. . . or hops

A lesser example of a compulsory marketing scheme is the Hops Board. It has reached the ultimate monopoly position of enforcing a rigid quota system. Even at the height of the BEMB it was still possible for newcomers to start egg production, and today farmers can still enter milk production. But it is illegal for a farmer to produce hops unless he owns or buys a quota. This watertight monopoly has survived only because the annual turnover of hops is a modest £7.5 million, a tiny proportion of the total cost of beer, the price of which is inflated by massive taxes.

The Hops Board may claim it has helped growers survive against cheaper hops from abroad, but it does not know how efficient British producers would be if faced with competition and relieved of the high price for quotas, which inflates costs. Growing bananas on expensive land in greenhouses in the middle of London is manifestly absurd, but is different only in degree from giving hopgrowers a monopoly so as to keep them in production.

. . . *but not chickens*

Those who criticize protectionist policies must explain the workings and benefits of a market economy. For over two decades I have engaged in three forms of agricultural production: milk, chicken meat (broilers), and eggs. Only chicken production was not "aided" by government. Behind my campaign to end the Egg Board was my anxiety to stop this old restrictive philosophy being applied to the new broiler industry.

In 1953, I started with a few hundred day-old chicks. Fifteen years later the resulting company was sold for more than £20 million. Assets can thus be created with little initial capital but a lot of initiative aided by the discovery procedure of competition. The final company, Allied Farm Foods, was created from more than seventy companies with about one hundred directors, of whom only five remained as directors although many others retained shareholdings. By 1968 annual sales exceeded £20 million and the value of each original Buxted £1 share had become about £550. Many investors (including me) made large sums of money in a business kept flexible by the absence of "government protection," and a new cheap food widened the choice of millions of consumers.

In the absence of well-meant government intervention, we were in direct and daily touch with our ultimate customer—the housewife—and had to bend every effort to meet her exacting requirements. Despite early criticisms about the taste of our chickens—by people who did not need to buy them—the business grew rapidly and became probably the most efficient form of agricultural production in the country. Quality improved and prices fell dramatically. I sold my first successful crop of chickens at 3 shillings 10 pence a pound in 1954. By 1968 the ex-farm price was down to 1 shilling 7½ pence, which was equivalent to 7½ pence after allowance for inflation. Meanwhile, the company's profits had risen to £1.7 million a year.

In this pioneering form of production, where there was so much to learn about new techniques, I was often reminded of Hayek's dictum that competition is the best discovery method. We soon had computers studying eight million chickens at a time on hundreds of farms, resulting in annual sales of some forty million birds. We experimented with many feedstuffs and ways of controlling disease. Experience led us to see the advantages of integration both vertically and horizontally. The flow of information from hundreds of farms helped us discover the most efficient methods and the best managers. Later I achieved a similar pooling of knowledge in three dairy farms I now manage without formal integration by exchanging costings and learning both from differences and similarities. Contrary to much that is thought (and taught in schools and universities), competition does not conflict with cooperation between producers for their mutual benefit.

If freed to follow a similar course, agriculture will become more integrated and more efficient. Individual farmers will prosper by using their abilities more effectively and learning from competition about feeding, breeding, and technological developments. This progress will be achieved if government sets about maximizing choice by getting out of the way of the farmer. Innovation and progress would be assisted more by lower taxes than by higher subsidies.

No profit without risk of loss

The story of Buxted Chickens is generally considered an

outstanding business success. "How easy to make money," some will say. But it is not always quite so simple as it appears looking back.

When in 1968 Buxted (then known as Allied Farm Foods) was taken over, I ventured into the plastic business. It came my way as a modest-sized venture so that in the event of failure the loss would be minimized. But as I have explained, economic progress is a continuing advance into the unknown. With the plastic company, high hopes swiftly turned into unforeseen problems and eventually complete failure. It is easy with hindsight to see the mistakes I made, but that does not reduce the loss which resulted.

Another business in which I was involved as an entrepreneur is concerned with the domestication of the green turtle in the Caribbean. In a company established in 1968 with the name "Mariculture," my business colleagues and I have had to learn not only how to feed and maintain the turtle, which was in danger of becoming extinct, but how to get it to breed in captivity. The purpose was to produce high quality meat, hide, oil, shell, and soup products and to market them on a commercial basis despite many obstacles, made worse by the well-intentioned efforts of conservationists who seek to bring the green turtle under protection as a threatened species.

We succeeded in breeding turtles in captivity. That is, we took eggs from the wild and reared them in captivity; we took turtles from the wild and managed to achieve mating and reproduction in captivity; and finally, the original turtle eggs which we hatched out in 1968 themselves mated in 1975. Technically, we may have succeeded, but financially we failed. It is said of a businessman that if he falls he can stand up again. But if he starts claiming that he has been pushed he is unlikely to be a successful businessman. With the turtle business we ran into a different kind of problem. Although by any standard it would surely seem that we were conserving turtles, there were those in the world of "conservation" who took a different view. On a number of occasions we established markets for our products at profitable prices, only to lose the markets because certain "conservationists" managed to get legislation passed prohibiting the sale of our product. The story is long and involved and in some cases almost unbelievable, but it is not for telling here. I think it would be fair to say that we had more friendly experts in the conservation world than we had enemies, but it only takes one man to change a law negatively and it may take a long time to get it changed back agan, although this in fact is what we did do. In the meantime capital reserves ran out. The business itself continues, but in other hands.

What of Europe?

The Common Agricultural Policy (CAP) of the EEC is nothing less than a monstrous international marketing board aimed at maintaining food prices above the world level to protect inefficient French and German farmers. History enables us to predict a massive distortion of trade, high prices, vast surpluses, and consequent waste of human and physical resources (i.e., losses), leading to mounting contradictions and demands for its abolition.

Even before the scandal of the butter mountain which was sold at a loss to Russia, surpluses of milk powder, cheese, and other dairy products were piling higher despite bonuses paid for exporting them. One example of economic distortion leading to further absurdities was butter exported from the CAP countries to Yugoslavia where it was converted into mayonnaise and exported back to the EEC. The mayonnaise was then put into a centrifuge to extract vinegar and parsley and, lo and behold, butter was reproduced ready for re-export by sharp businessmen!

Other scandals have been even less honest. Since the Vatican is not within the EEC, sugar exported from Rome to the Vatican received a subsidy. This artificial barrier opened up profitable possibilities for traders. Not surprisingly, it was found that the residents of the Vatican were apparently eating large quantities of sugar—some seven pounds per person per day! Similarly, large quantities of grain have moved to and fro up the EEC rivers, not being discharged but just collecting bonuses *en route*. No one should be surprised at such consequences of faking the price system by arbitrary subsidies.

High prices for producers under CAP inevitably lead to excess supplies which hang over the market and must make farmers uncertain about the future. If government would only withdraw, efficient farmers would prosper and the industry would continually be readjusting itself like any progressive industry which must take account of new demands, technical changes, consumer preferences, greater knowledge, and better techniques.

Well-meant intervention once again produces damaging consequences which further distort activity in the countries to which the surpluses are exported at prices below their true costs of production. Senator Hubert Humphrey, formerly a U.S. presidential candidate, told a London audience in 1971 of the damage CAP has done to American agricultural markets.

> In practice CAP has become a major disruptive force in world agricultural markets. One reason is that its price levels are so far above world market levels. Another reason is that price relationships within the CAP system are set in . . . such a way as to favor the use of expensive home products in place of lower-priced imports. For example, soft wheat grown in the Common Market is increasingly used to substitute for imported corn in feeding animals. . . .
>
> Estimates by the U.S. Department of Agriculture put the cost of the national farm support program . . . of the European Community at about $5,000 million a year. This must be added to the roughly $3,000 million that is spent each year under the CAP program jointly managed from Brussels. But these are not the only costs. The high prices maintained by the CAP program probably cost consumers in the Common Market another $6,000 million to $7,000 million a year over and above what they would pay if food were available at world market prices. This in turn releases strong inflationary forces, obliging workers to fight for higher and higher wages to cover their weekly food bill.[2]

SOCIAL "WELFARE"

Not even the most complacent apologist for British politicians would deny that the combined record of Labor and Conservative economic and social policies since 1945 has fallen tragically short of the high hopes of all the politicians in power during that period. What went wrong?

Postwar paradoxes

Clearly there has been no shortage of good intentions as party men have competed with one another to promise voters all they could possibly wish. Nor can failure be blamed on lack of government control over the economy. Indeed, the striking feature of public policy since the war has been the consistency with which politicians, irrespective of philosophy, have met almost every problem or setback with the claim that more taxation or more government control would put things right. With the exception of Churchill's administration after 1951, which "set the people free" from the remnants of wartime restrictions with visibly beneficial results, the drift has been towards increasing control by politicians and civil servants who have taken more and more decisions away from taxpayers, consumers, and businessmen. In short, the trend has been towards minimizing individual choice.

Increasing taxation, mounting legislation, spreading welfare, sprawling subsidies, creeping—and sometimes galloping—nationalization, have led to repeated panics, particularly under the two Labor governments which both devalued the pound (in 1949 and 1967), and have now led to an inflation without precedent in modern British history, even in time of war.

Among many bewildering paradoxes in these twenty-eight years, three are noteworthy. The first is that never before have democratic politicians sought popularity with such unprincipled singlemindedness; and yet opinion polls show they have never been held in lower popular esteem. The practice of expediency has clearly proved highly inexpedient. The second is that although inflation has followed from the intensification of controls—over resources, location of industry, education, training, investment, prices, and incomes—the only "remedy" a Conservative government could think of in 1972 was more of the same disastrous medicine. The third paradox is that as politicians have armed themselves with more power, they appear increasingly powerless to achieve any of their purposes. Prices rise faster, the floating pound sinks, grievances multiply, and the welfare state produces anything but a state of welfare.

A year before Mr. Heath replaced Mr. Wilson, Peregrine Worsthorne wrote of the Conservative opposition:

> At the moment, they are offering the same kind of basic prospectus as Harold Wilson offered in 1964—a change of hands on the levers controlling the domestic economy.
> . . .

Except for a brief interlude after their 1970 victory, the Conservatives followed policies barely distinguishable from the choice-reducing program of the Labor government.

Adam Smith, again

By 1970, with such a large proportion of national activity outside the market, economic cause and effect were difficult to relate. The decision-makers no longer receive the playback from their decisions. Those in charge of a company in a free market receive rapid reactions to their many decisions. Bad decisions swiftly produce trouble and either the policies or the men in charge are changed. In monopolistic government activities, bad decisions are insulated from the self-correcting discipline of the market.

In the *Wealth of Nations,* Adam Smith foresaw the danger which he hoped might be avoided by keeping government in bounds:

> . . . though the profusion of government must, undoubtedly, have retarded the natural progress of England towards wealth and improvement, it has not been able to stop it. . . . In the midst of all the exactions of government,

capital has been silently and gradually accumulated by the private frugality and good conduct of individuals, by their universal, continual, and uninterrupted effort to better their own condition. It is this effort, protected by law and allowed by liberty to exert itself in the manner that is most adv.4 tageous, which has maintained the progress of England towards opulence and improvement in almost all former times and which, it is to be hoped, will do so in all future times.

England however, as it has never been blessed with a very parsimonious government, so parsimony has at no time been the characteristical virtue of its inhabitants. It is the highest impertinence and presumption, therefore, in kings and ministers, to pretend to watch over the economy of private people, and to restrain their expense, either by sumptuary laws, or by prohibiting the importation of foreign luxuries. They are themselves always, and without any exception, the greatest spendthrifts in the society.[3]

A contemporary example of this process at work two hundred years after Adam Smith wrote is provided by the nationalized industries. Between 1955 and 1970 their net income as a percentage of net assets ranged between 2.2 and 5.8 compared with the equivalent figures for private industry of 12 and 17.4. Mr. George Polanyi has given the following contrast in price performance, without taking account of the many hidden subsidies to the railways and coalmines.

Between 1951 and 1964 the average price rise of the products of the nationalized industries was 95 per cent, yet in private manufacturing industry the increase averaged only 18 per cent over the same period. Between October 1964 and March 1970 the figures were 32 per cent for nationalized products and 27 per cent for all products, so that inflation owes as much to the nationalized industries as our export success owes to private enterprise.[4]

Do not many of these confusions arise from the false assumption that work (or investment) necessarily creates wealth when in practice it may be misdirected and lead to losses which reduce wealth? Wealth is only the consequence of mutually advantageous voluntary exchange. If the government sets about maximizing voluntary exchange, wealth will be created at the fastest rate. If this maximum-exchange theory is correct, we should welcome the extension of pricing. When restrictions are applied to foreign exchanges, such as exchange control, compulsion obliterates or falsifies these indicators. The signposts are then wrong and travelers will take wrong turnings as surely as an airplane pilot will crash if he is misled by false instruments. If all road signs were turned in random directions, the more energetically travelers walked, ran, or drove, the worse the muddle and the more the waste of energy. It would be no use blaming the resulting disorders on people being more lazy or less competent than elsewhere.

25 pence in the pound

A major part of Britain's economic activity where good intentions have led to a most damaging misdirection of effort and expenditure is in the so-called welfare state. Before examining its inefficiency as a means of redistributing income to help the poor, let us remind ourselves that it now accounts for almost half total public expenditure and therefore about one-quarter of the national income. In other words almost twenty-five new pennies in every pound of British income is channelled through central and local government to pay for state education, medical care, housing, pensions, and other social benefits.

Let us note that while there is still no shortage of privately produced color television sets, automobiles, kitchen equipment, cameras, or hi-fi equipment, government-provided welfare services are riddled with shortage of doctors, teachers, hospital beds, council (and rent-restricted) housing, modern schools, and even state pensions sufficient for the needs of the poorest. The explanation in brief is that these welfare services are provided by state monopolies that lack the check and challenge of competing suppliers. They are financed by the public not as consumers who choose to pay prices which cover (inflated) costs, but as taxpayers who have no choice to take their money elsewhere. Choice is confined to those who are sufficiently rich to pay twice—once as conscripted taxpayers and again as paying customers for an alternative private school or health service. So we see the double damage done by state welfare services: first as monopolies which are shielded from the spur to efficiency provided by competition, and second as suppliers of "free" or subsidized services which are therefore insulated from the test of consumer choice.

Such an inefficient, choice-denying apparatus as nationalized welfare might be justified if it proved a method of giving a good bargain at least to families with low incomes who might otherwise not be able to afford essential welfare services. A study of official statistics removes this last pretext from the defenders of compulsory state-financed welfare.

Part of the explanation for this surprising state of affairs was given by Mr. Arthur Shenfield in an essay entitled "Trial by Taxation";[5] under the heading "Helping the Poor?" he wrote:

> The redistribution of incomes has this remarkable feature, that the majority of both its champions and its opponents believe that it happens in a sense that it does not. . . . The reason is that though our system does indeed tax the rich exceptionally heavily, the magnitude of the total effect is misconceived. There simply are not enough rich to make much difference. . . . The modern high-taxing, high-spending state does not obtain its vast revenues from the rich but from heavy taxes on all citizens, including the poor.

Even if we ignore the hidden inefficiency of monopoly state welfare and the effect of the resulting high taxes in inflating wage claims, it must be clear that the national balance-sheet shows a large net loss on welfare services which account for almost a quarter of total national income. Here is evidence to convince the most skeptical that the substitution of compulsion for individual choice impoverishes even those it is most intended to benefit. Its harmful effects run far wider than the inefficient provision of social welfare; high taxation does damage to efficiency and economy.

More choice for more welfare

So far from government compulsion being necessary to ensure adequate expenditure on essential welfare services, the evidence shows that even with massive state spending, the standards in education, medical care, council housing, and basic pensions are falling further behind the levels families insist on in their homes, clothing, food, holidays, and personal amenities which are all supplied at competitive prices in the market. Subject to minimum requirements and government help for those in need, private provision of these welfare services would lead to more rapidly rising standards.

If consumers were free to choose between competing welfare suppliers, they would insist on better value for their money and be prepared to pay more (voluntarily) from their own pockets than they can be induced to pay (compulsorily) in higher taxes for government services. Some Conservative politicians used to talk as if they understood this truly humane case for choice in welfare. Experience after 1964 taught at least two leading Labor ministers the weakness of looking to increased taxation as the way to improve welfare services.

The first was Mr. Douglas Houghton whom Mr. Wilson put in charge of coordinating Labor's social policy on pensions, health, and education. Drawing on this experience, he wrote in 1967 that

> While people would be willing to pay for better services for themselves, they may not be willing to pay more in taxes as a kind of insurance premium which may bear no relation to the services actually received.
>
> . . . from the standpoint of the quality and efficiency and the adequacy of the services, we are now getting the

worst of both worlds. The government cannot find the money out of taxation and the citizen is not allowed to pay it out of his own pocket . . . there are valid objections to the state bearing out of general taxation almost the full cost of personal services which many citizens could well afford to pay for if not actually to provide for themselves.[6]

The other Labor leader who at least glimpsed the light was Mr. Richard Crossman when in 1969 he launched a White Paper on national superannuation which included the following significant passage:

> . . . people are prepared to subscribe more in a contribution for their own personal or family security than they would ever be willing to pay in taxation devoted to a wide variety of different purposes.[7]

Who said a "swindle"?

Perhaps a last word from two ministers of social security may remove any vestige of doubt that the present system of state welfare is very different from the noble ideal which Beveridge taught the postwar generation to believe. In a book entitled *The Great Pensions "Swindle,"* [8] Mr. Arthur Seldon drew special attention to the word *swindle* as having been used by both Labor and Conservative ministers to describe the finance of state retirement pensions. Thus in 1959 Mr. Crossman, speaking for the Labor opposition, described the Conservative proposals put forward by Mr. John Boyd-Carpenter as follows:

> I think those of us who on first reading described the White Paper as a counterfeit or bogus imitation of the Labor Party's plan were understating how bad it was. On reflection, we now realize that if we were to call this bill a swindle we would not be exaggerating. . . .[9]

Ten years later when Mr. Crossman's proposals were being debated in the House of Commons it was Mr. Boyd-Carpenter's turn for the Conservative opposition.

. . . if those who were responsible for that [1959 Conservative] scheme were responsible for a swindle, it was a very small peccadillo compared with the scale of swindling operations for which the right Hon. Gentleman [Mr. Crossman] is responsible.[10]

When the political debate between leading experts on state welfare degenerates into a question of how big a swindle its financing really is, the case for radical reform to restore individual choice surely becomes irresistible. A reduction in universal subsidies would increase choice, first, for the better-off majority by reducing taxation and, second, for the really poor minority by more generous assistance, perhaps in the form of vouchers.[11]

GOVERNMENT SPENDING AND INFLATION

Although state welfare is the largest area over which individual choice is more or less suppressed by centralized political decision, all taxation is a denial of voluntary exchange between willing buyer and willing seller where both gain from the transaction. Some idea of the reduction in choice from this source is conveyed by the proportion of total national income spent by central and local government; although there are more ways than one of measuring such magnitudes and inflation quickly renders any monetary totals out of date.

From the *Financial Statement,* we can work out that total public expenditure planned for 1973-4 was about £32,000 million while all forms of taxation amounted to about £27,600 million, leaving a deficit (described by the treasury as the "borrowing requirement") of £4,400 million. If we put the total national income in 1973 money values at around £55,000 million, we can see that public spending accounts for well over half of all spending. The result is not only high taxation which reduces individual choice, but also the piling up of pressures which make for inflation.

In 1945 Dr. Colin Clark concluded from extensive study that where taxation (plus government deficits) exceeded 25 per cent of the national income, then forces were set in motion which resulted, not immediately but within two or three years, in a general rise in costs and prices.[12]

Almost twenty years later he brought his researches up to date and found that countries with the best record on inflation (then including Japan and Switzerland) had kept taxes below his critical level of 25 per cent. Dr. Clark's general explanation of the cause-and-effect link between high taxes and rising prices was as follows:

> . . . taxation raises costs partly through discouraging productive effort; more significantly, perhaps, in causing industrialists to become careless about costs (if half of any increase in costs is "on the treasury," they will make much less effort to avoid it, whether it be a wage increase, interest charges, or an expense account) and, finally and in rather a subtle manner, the existence of a high level of taxation alters the whole climate of politics: politicians tend to lose their capacity to resist pressures, whether governmental or private, leading to cost increases, in the more or less unconscious knowledge that a rise in prices will lower the real value of all fixed charges on the budget and in that way lighten their burden.[13]

Since Colin Clark wrote these words, the record of Labor and Conservative governments almost exactly illustrates this irresponsible attitude towards costly gambles. If high taxation leads to carelessness in public and private spending, it follows that the poor value for money received by government has the effect of diluting its value.

It is interesting that a similar finding has been reached by Mr. Ronald Burgess working independently on accountancy lines at the Economic Study Association. In November 1971, he wrote:

> My own work on local government finance has led me to the conclusion that in any given situation there is a definite limit to public income and that public expenditure must be adjusted to this limit.[14]

Money and the unions

Mr. Heath maintained that the cause of inflation lies in the power of trade unions to enforce excessive wage demands. Certainly the trade unions have too much power, but if government did not prop up public and private lame ducks, spend vast sums of taxpayers' money uneconomically, and stifle competition in all its forms, the trade unions would have less scope to inflate money wages and more prospects of increased real wages. The impact of progressive tax rates on take-home pay means that wage increases of perhaps 12 or 14 per cent are needed to offset an increase in prices of 10 per cent.

When inflation exceeds 20 per cent a year and taxes rise steeply, standards of living must fall. Over a two-year period inflation will be over 40 per cent. Therefore, over that two-year period a worker should receive over 40 per cent increase in wages and to achieve this, with taxes in excess of 30 per cent, he requires a salary raise of about 80 to 100 per cent to achieve anything at all. No wonder the country is beset with problems! The only beneficiary of inflation is the government.

Certainly legislation is necessary to make unions subject to contract and put an end to intimidation and compulsion, but the most logical reason for not blaming inflation on them has been stated by Professor Milton Friedman, who has summarized[15] much historical research as follows:

> It is easy to show that the widely held union-wage-push theory of inflation is not correct. If A is *the* cause of B, then whenever A occurs, B will also occur, and whenever B occurs, so will A. *Trade unions* (A) were as strong in the U.S. in 1961-64, when there was no *inflation* (B), as in 1965-69, when there was inflation. Prices in the U.S. more than doubled in the Civil War, when unions were almost nonexistent, in World War I, when unions were weak, and in World War II when unions were strong. Prices in the U.S. rose more than 30 per cent from 1849 to

1857, and again from 1895 to 1914, both periods when unions were extremely weak.

Inflation has plagued countries with negligible trade unions and with strong trade unions; and both kinds of countries have had periods of price stability.

So we return to Colin Clark's central finding. But if excessive taxation creates conditions that favor a general rise in costs and prices, this effect can be sustained over a period only if governments obligingly increase the circulation of money to finance a similar volume of transactions at higher monetary values.

Friedman, who places primary blame for inflation on lax monetary policy, and Colin Clark, who blames taxation, strongly reinforce each other when we look at British public finances. Despite a record level of taxation in 1974, the chancellor of the exchequer ran a deficit of over £4,000 million to catch up with a runaway expenditure of £32,000 million. Both Friedman[16] and Clark would agree that the financing of this deficit with the help of the printing press and newly-created credit must lead to inflation. So long as monetary inflation is being stoked up, no prices and incomes policy can stop the effect working its way through, first into the uncontrolled sector of foodstuffs, land, housing, gold, antiques, and then throughout the economy as the controls are relaxed or evaded or completely overwhelmed by the pent-up pressure of monetary demand.

Twenty years ago a private banker with firsthand experience of the great German inflation of 1923 warned British politicians that they were heading, however gradually, in precisely the same direction. In his forthright evidence to the Radcliffe Commission on money and credit (1957),[17] Mr. Walter Salomon summarized the central cause and main cures of inflation as follows:

Inflation has persisted for twelve years after the end of the war primarily because the state plays too large a part in economic activity. This has made the supply of money larger than it should have been and the output of goods and services smaller than it could have been. The solutions lie in reducing public expenditure, tightening control over the supply of money and credit, reducing taxation, offering stronger incentives to effort and saving, and revitalizing industry by reasserting the authority of the owners and restoring competition.

I have expressed much the same thing in criticizing policies that minimize private choice. If Mr. Salomon and the academics I have quoted here agree that this centralization of decisions is the basic source of inflation, then here is another devil we may hope to exorcise by restoring choice (along with a large part of taxation) back to the individual who will insist on better value in spending his own money.

Compulsion reduces satisfaction

The general argument is that by exchanging goods or services freely, and receiving something they value more in return for what they give, people *increase* the total value of *all* the goods and services available as a whole.

It must also follow, of course, that people who are *forced* to exchange do not benefit in the same way. The assumption is that if they had stood to gain they would not have needed to be forced to exchange. And compulsory exchange includes the payment of taxes (or national insurance contributions) for the services supplied by central or local government. All one can say is that they are likely to be valued less, and probably much less, than the money they have had taken away from them in taxes. Compulsion must reduce the satisfaction individuals derive from their incomes.

In other words, the vast amount of money spent on "public services," and on government itself, may be worth much less than the value on paper shown in terms of pounds. Yet "public expenditure" is included in the national income as though it were worth as much as the values created by voluntary exchange. There could be no greater fallacy. A pound spent by a civil servant does *not* add as much value as a pound spent by a person backing his own judgment and bettering his condition. Government may be, for some activities, a necessary evil; but it is a bad substitute for voluntary exchange wherever free markets can be allowed to function.

Hope from Indonesia

From an abundance of evidence, let me conclude with an unexpected example of the practical application of my principle about maximizing choice from Indonesia. It will be found in an official publication of the International Monetary Fund (IMF).[18] After years of Marxist dictatorship in Indonesia, inflation speeded up in the early 1960s until by mid-1966 prices were rising at an annual rate of more than 1,500 per cent. The Marxists were overthrown in a bloody revolution and by October 1966 the new government was ready to launch a very different policy based essentially on freeing individual choice from communist-style controls.

The following record is an abbreviated account which relies as far as possible on the words used in the IMF report to describe the principles pursued and their consequences. The basic change was "away from a government-dominated economy towards a system in which market forces played a predominant role." This new approach led the government to "curtail less essential budget expenditures and to eliminate the large operational losses of many public sector enterprises." Abroad came the introduction of "an exchange system virtually free of restrictions on payments, with flexible exchange rates for most transactions." The budget was balanced by 1968 and a firmer grip was taken on monetary policy. From 760 per cent in 1966, the rate of increase in the money supply fell to 120 per cent in 1968 and 60 per cent in 1969. Where stabilization was expected to take many years, the remarkable consequences of this about-face in policy were seen by 1969 when the rate of inflation had fallen from 1,500 to 10 per cent.

Did the result support what the IMF report calls "the popular belief that stabilization needs to entail economic stagnation or recession''? This is how the question was answered in its own words:

> Although comprehensive statistics are not available, import and export data as well as other indicators strongly suggest that the stabilization period was marked by a substantial *increase* in economic activity. . . .
>
> Provided that available resources are allocated primarily on the basis of economic criteria, stabilization can indeed proceed simultaneously with economic growth. [My emphasis.]

No wonder the report concludes that ''the Indonesian program represents a promising model of anti-inflationary policies.''

Warning from the Common Market

We have already glimpsed some of the absurdities of the EEC as it restricts choice for producers and consumers in agriculture. Whatever the theory or wider hopes for British membership in the EEC, one of the commissioners, Dr. Ralf Dahrendorf, warned against it. In *The Times*[19] he was reported as saying that the commission has become

> . . . an illiberal and bureaucratic leviathan obsessed with harmonizing things just for the sake of harmonization.
> . . .

For hundreds of years an Englishman has been considered innocent until proved guilty and still enjoys freedom to appeal to higher courts. In Brussels the only court to which an Englishman accused by the commission of breaking one of the countless proliferating regulations may appeal is the European Court of Justice. Sir Henry Slessor (a former Labor solicitor general) wrote to *The Times*,[20] warning that European justice is not the same as British justice:

> As a Lord Justice of Appeal (retired) and a member of the Judicial Committee of the Privy Council I venture to call

the attention of your readers to a fact which, in my view, differentiates the United Kingdom in a very essential matter from the whole Continent.

The laws of England, those of the United States, the Dominions and those now independent Afro-Asian states (the last through the education of their leaders and the universal decisions of the Privy Council) were and are based on the libertarian principles of the Common Law.

In contrast the European system of Roman Law is based on the didactic codified edicts of authority, derived from Justinian and Napoleon.

This is not merely a juristic difference but also a fundamental divergence of outlook; the one favoring freedom, and the other emphasizing authority.

England has never been a part of Europe since the departure of the Romans; even Charlemagne did not include England in the Holy Roman Empire.

In *The Daily Telegraph*[21] a month later, Ronald Bell, MP, QC, commented:

This Treaty of 248 Articles is abstract, jealous, pedantic, and more pervasive than is commonly realized. There is little that does not come within the range of ensuring fair competition, even recipes for beer, wine, and sauces, the shape of bottles, working hours and conditions. Brussels has the power to rule almost all except defense and foreign policy, and within about five years will be largely doing so. . . .

Without realizing it the British public has been led along a path which must lead even more rapidly to less choice. The giving up of Magna Carta and the Bill of Rights is a major issue and not just the tearing up of scraps of paper. How does all this come about? As always when choice is minimized, it happens slowly, slowly, without the victims realizing the implications.

In his *Anatomy of Britain*,[22] Anthony Sampson gives his judgment:

. . . the most drastic bypass of parliament has been the most important of all post-war issues—the question of joining the Common Market. When the Treaty of Rome was prepared in 1957, none of the European parliaments was able to discuss it in detail: the treaty itself had been drafted by delegates from each country, who spent several months with their civil servants, negotiating and working out the complicated technical questions of tariffs, capital movement, agriculture. The treaty was then put forward to the parliaments virtually as a *fait accompli,* to be either rejected or ratified as a whole. The arrangements were far too technical to be left to ordinary parliamentarians: faced with a take-it-or-leave-it proposition, they reluctantly took it.

The dangers were emphasized by Oxford economist Peter Oppenheimer when he took a forward look at the commission's efforts to achieve "harmonization":

In technical matters harmonization is unobjectionable but the commission will not stop here. In the long run it is bound to turn its attention to such areas as professional qualifications and recruitment methods, organization of public services, school and university structure and a host of other matters. Where others see the cultural diversity of Europe, the Common Market Commission sees only distortions in the labor market and unfair competitive advantage.

"Harmonizing" Europe will mean destroying much of this cultural diversity and transforming the Continent into a bureaucratic parade-ground. How ironic if the gentlemen in Brussels are able to destroy in the next generation what Soviet tanks on one side and Coca-Cola on the other have allowed to escape in our own day![23]

Free trade puts the whole of the United Kingdom at the center of world trade—where it used to be when it was prosperous. In the

Common Market, the United Kingdom and especially Scotland, Northern Ireland, and of course, Southern Italy and Sicily, become areas of low economic potential. The Common Market is supposed to be a free trade area. In fact, it is a confusion of government controls, restrictions and red tape and has put a huge tariff barrier around one of the areas of densest population in the world. This can only be harmful.

The United States

Since the United States economy is the largest and the most successful so far evolved by man, much can be learned from American experience. The key lesson is that past success has not prevented the syndrome from appearing. The incredible wealth of the U.S.A. after the Second World War made it seem that their riches were unlimited and they could do what they liked. One consequence was ever-increasing government expenditure, some of it in a bewildered endeavor to put most of the rest of the world onto a sound economic footing by one form of subsidy or another. Added to this expenditure was the burden of the Vietnam War and mounting extravagance of the Great Society programs, in a vain effort to hasten the millennium.

Such over-spending could have been expected to produce inflationary consequences, including balance-of-payments deficits, and it promptly did. By 1969 it could be foreseen that even a Republican administration would endeavor to "hold" prices and wages with controls. At the end of 1970 President Nixon was pleading with business and labor to try to restrain price increases and wage demands, while pumping more money into the economy.

About this time Professor Milton Friedman visited London and was interviewed by the *Sunday Times*.[24] Asked if the impression was correct that he regarded inflation as the greatest economic evil, he replied:

No. Inflation *per se* is not a good thing but it is not the greatest economic evil. The greatest economic evil arises out of the measures that are mistakenly used to combat inflation like pegging exchange rates and seeking to influence wages and prices through incomes policies, freezes and other forms of control . . . if you have open inflation it is perfectly possible for people to adjust to it. They will come to expect it. Interest rates will go up, wages will escalate. The market can operate to enable individuals through private transactions to allocate resources and organize economic activity.

On the other hand, if you repress price movements, if you hold particular prices or wages fixed, you destroy the market mechanism. You must have something in its place. What gets put in its place is either chance, favoritism, bribery, or governmental control. We have ample experience that these methods are highly inefficient. May I say also that the pretended cures are not cures. I know of no inflation at any time, anywhere, which has ever been cured by wage or price control or freeze.

Must Diocletian's lesson be learned again by bitter experience, after "much blood [was] shed on trifling account"?

5
What Can Be Done
EXAMPLES OF THEORY IN ACTION

The main threads of my argument have been that individuals are not powerless victims of fate; that history proves we can do something to avert recurrent disaster; and that if we act with understanding of natural forces or principles, the improvement in our economic fortunes could be dramatic and sustained. Against the background of a dangerous drift to disaster in the postwar years, I now want to set out some of my experience over this period that may encourage rational hopes for the future.

At the end of the war I was very troubled about whether the deaths and other sacrifices would once again fail to bring freedom, prosperity, and lasting peace. The omens of the 1945 General Election did not strike me as very promising. What I would now call the minimizing of individual choice by the Labor government made me even more pessimistic about the direction party politics seemed to be taking us.

Birth of the IEA

About this time, I read a shortened verion[1] of Professor Hayek's *Road to Serfdom* and was so impressed that I bought the book and sought out the author. It was for me a fateful meeting. My central question was what, if anything, he could advise me to do to help get discussion and policy on the right lines. I do not recall his exact words but have retained almost thirty years later a vivid impression of his message. Hayek first warned against wasting time—as I was then tempted—by taking up a political career. He explained his view that the decisive influence in the great battle of ideas and policy was wielded by the intellectuals whom he characterized as the "second-hand dealers in ideas."[2] It was the dominant intellectuals from the Fabians onward who had tilted the political debate in favor of growing government intervention with all that followed. If I shared the view that better ideas were not getting a fair hearing, his counsel was that I should join with others in forming a scholarly research organization to supply intellectuals in universities, schools, journalism, and broadcasting with authoritative studies of the economic theory of markets and its application to practical affairs.

In 1953 I started my chicken business and by 1955 felt sufficiently hopeful of the financial prospects to form an educational trust with the title Institute of Economic Affairs (IEA).

A footnote in *The Road to Serfdom*[3] on exchange controls inspired the first venture into publication of the embryonic IEA.

> The extent of the control over all life that economic control confers is nowhere better illustrated than in the field of foreign exchanges. Nothing would at first seem to affect private life less than a state control of the dealings in foreign exchange, and most people will regard its introduction with complete indifference. Yet the experience of most continental countries has taught thoughtful people to regard this step as the decisive advance on the path to totalitarianism and the suppression of individual liberty.
>
> It is in fact the complete delivery of the individual to the tyranny of the state, the final suppression of all means of escape—not merely for the rich, but for everybody. Once the individual is no longer free to travel, no longer free to buy foreign books or journals, once all the means of foreign contact can be restricted to those of whom official opinion approves or for whom it is regarded as necessary, the effective control of opinion is much greater than that ever exercised by any of the absolutist governments of the seventeenth and eighteenth centuries.

As an experiment, I commissioned a free-lance economic journalist, Mr. George Winder, to write *The Free Convertibility of Sterling*. It was published by Batchworth Press in 1956 at the cost of £200 for 2,000 copies. The first intellectual to respond was Henry Hazlitt, who devoted his regular column in *Newsweek* to an enthusiastic review. Orders came in from around the world and over the following years I was to meet many readers of George Winder's little classic as evidence of Hayek's process of long-term education at work.

Thus encouraged, I got in touch with Ralph Harris who by 1956, at the age of thirty-one, had finished seven years teaching at St. Andrews University and had moved to the *Glasgow Herald* as an editorial writer. In January 1957, on the promise of £1,000 in the bank, he agreed to come to London as General Director (and sole employee) of the Institute of Economic Affairs in a small city office rented for £3 a week. At last there was the beginning of what might now be called a "think tank" with the difference that it was as independent of politics as of business or any other interest. Helped by an advisory council which included Sir Oscar Hobson, Colin Clark, Professor Eric Nash, Graham Hutton, and George Schwartz, its purpose, as set out in early publications, was

> . . . to foster public understanding of how economic principles can illumine the great public issues of the day and in particular to examine economic policies by reference to the requirements of a free society.

Among its early publications were studies of pensions, trade unions, advertising, hire purchase, the City of London's earnings, the sterling problem, and monetary policy which certainly had consequences at the intellectual level though they taught lessons for policy that have still not been fully learned twenty years later. The first author Ralph Harris commissioned was another first-class economist, London School of Economics-trained Arthur Seldon, who after writing *Pensions in a Free Society* promptly joined the IEA in 1958 and has ever since been its editorial director. In 1959 they recruited two secretaries and moved to a basement office at Hobart Place, which gave its name to the IEA's most famous series, the *Hobart Papers*.

Call for freedom

Meanwhile, I had drawn further encouragement from an international group of scholars, writers, and more thoughtful businessmen which also owed its inspiration to Professor Hayek. In April 1947, he had invited leading liberal economists and philosophers to a private conference at Mont Pelerin, near Vevey in Switzerland, from which has grown the Mont Pelerin Society (MPS). Its aim as drafted by Hayek and approved by those attending that first meeting, may be worth quoting for reflection more than twenty-five years later.

A group of economists, historians, philosophers, and other students of public affairs from Europe and the United States met at Mont Pelerin, Switzerland, from April 1st to 10th, 1947, to discuss the crisis of our times. This group, being desirous of perpetuating its existence for promoting further intercourse and for inviting the collaboration of other like-minded persons, has agreed upon the following statement of aims.

The central values of civilization are in danger. Over large stretches of the earth's surface the essential conditions of human dignity and freedom have already disappeared. In others they are under constant menace from the development of current tendencies of policy.

The position of the individual and the voluntary group are progressively undermined by extensions of arbitrary power. Even that most precious possession of Western Man, freedom of thought and expression, is threatened by the spread of creeds which, claiming the privilege of tolerance when in the position of a minority, seek only to establish a position of power in which they can suppress and obliterate all views but their own.

The group holds that these developments have been fostered by the growth of a view of history which denies all absolute moral standards and by the growth of theories which question the desirability of the rule of law. It holds further that they have been fostered by a decline of belief in private property and the competitive market; for without the diffused power and initiative associated with these institutions, it is difficult to imagine a society in which freedom may be effectively preserved. . . . The group does not aspire to conduct propaganda. It seeks to establish no meticulous and hampering orthodoxy. It aligns itself with no particular party. Its object is solely, by facilitating the exchange of views among minds inspired by certain ideals and broad conceptions held in common, to contribute to the preservation and improvement of the free society.

In the early 1950s I met Karl Brandt, professor of agricultural economics at Stanford University. He invited me to visit California, an invitation I readily accepted. He was to open my eyes as to the tremendous possibilities for specialized agriculture. He himself was a remarkable man. In 1953 I received an invitation from him to give a talk to the Mont Pelerin Society at its meeting in September 1954 in Venice. My subject was to be The Government and Agriculture. I believe that he had met few, if any, farmers who were prepared to make a case that government aid to farmers was likely to be counter-productive. I accepted the invitation and had a most enjoyable meeting, the first of many. Amongst the other people I met there was Professor Ludwig von Mises, who I am sure will go down in the annals of history as one of the greatest economists of all. I also met Arthur Shenfield for the first time.

In 1959 Ralph Harris helped organize the 10th International Conference of the MPS at Oxford where leading British economists associated with the IEA (including Graham Hutton, John Jewkes, Herbert Frankel, Basil Yamey, Peter Bauer, S. R. Dennison) were able to renew links that were to bear much fruit with such outstanding European and American scholars as

Wilhelm Röpke, Milton Friedman, George Stigler, Ludwig Erhard, Fritz Machlup, Karl Brandt, James Buchanan, Gottfried Haberler, Trygve Hoff, W. H. Hutt, Frank Knight, and Jacques Rueff.

The case of rpm . . .

In January 1960, the institute published its first Hobart Paper, a critical study of resale price maintenance (rpm) by Professor B. S. Yamey. I recall asking Ralph Harris why he thought a study of such an apparently dull, little-noticed subject was worth producing. I have never forgotten his answer, which was that the argument was "so well documented, scholarly and convincing." With hindsight, it is easy to understand why rpm had not previously been dealt with, either by a trade association, trade union, or political party. It was a restrictive practice designed to help sellers by confining consumer choice to fixed prices for branded products. Only a completely independent organization could risk offending such a powerful lobby as the small shopkeepers, who traditionally had come to think of rpm as a protection against more efficient forms of retailing.

Four years later Mr. Edward Heath, who as president of the Board of Trade was piloting a bill through the House of Commons to end rpm, lunched at the institute and met Basil Yamey. He pointed to him, saying, "You are the cause of all my trouble." The "trouble" was the political fracas in his own party as well as from Labor MPs, trade associations, and some manufacturers who felt threatened by the restoration of competitive prices. It may have been politically inexpedient to take this action a few months before the 1964 election, but it certainly contributed to the reforming reputation of Mr. Heath which propelled him into the leadership of the Tory Party the following year.

Here was a classic example of a scholar working without any political power, ambition, or intent, having a practical effect through attracting the attention of reviewers, civil servants, and finally men of action. Subsequently, a mutual friend who knew Mr. Heath well told me how he tried to get Mr. Heath at the Board of Trade to tackle another pressing problem but Mr. Heath explained that, having the choice between two reforms, he went for rpm because the case was fully documented. Here was tangible proof of Hayek's view that scholarly research should take pride of place over political campaigning.

The success of Hobart Paper I as a student text was proved by the publication of four editions within as many years after its first appearance.

A frequent criticism of the IEA approach to education is that its publications do not reach the masses. But they are aimed at a different "market," namely Hayek's "intellectuals," who as teachers and writers retail ideas for wider consumption. Their strength is based on the belief that the scholar who understands his subject best and can convince his peers, will have the most effect, though it will often take longer than four years to win through.

. . . and nuclear energy

It has been the experience of the IEA that when a study is authoritative, logical, clearly written, and avoids political partisanship, it will attract attention in press, radio, and television and will be noticed by civil servants and MPs of all political colors.

Since 1957 the IEA has published works by about two hundred authors of diverse political allegiances and of none, on aspects of market pricing and competition in a wide range of goods and services, whether supplied by private or public enterprise, including welfare, roads, telephones, postal services, currencies, and savings. An important example was Research Monograph 9, *The Political Economy of Nuclear Energy,* written by an independent economic consultant, Professor Duncan Burn. The disappointing result of nuclear power in Britain controlled by the monopolistic Atomic Energy Authority was contrasted with the success of the U.S. Atomic Energy Commission which from the start encouraged competition and private enterprise. The original mistake was traced back to 1941 when expert scientists advised the government that such an important potential must "not be allowed to fall into the hands of private business." From this restriction of choice followed the sorry story summarized in a half-page review in the *Daily Mirror*[4] which lamented: "Britain no longer leads the world in putting the atom to work."[5]

By an interesting coincidence, while lecturing in the U.S.A., I met in Dallas, Texas, the man responsible for American atomic energy policy. He was an attorney who on returning after the war decided that it was dangerous for government to have a monopoly of nuclear power and set about doing something about it. Naturally, I was interested and requested more information. Working as a private citizen, he prepared plans to balance private initiative with the necessary framework of government control. Over a period of ten years, Congress enacted a number of laws culminating in an act permitting the private ownership of nuclear materials in the same manner as gas, oil, and coal. In retrospect, this creative process blossomed due to one individual—a private, nonpolitical person—acting early in a well-thought-out manner to preserve the discovery procedure of competition on the grounds that no government agency can produce an Einstein.

The lesson we can learn is that laws being passed today have their origins many years ago. My story illustrates that, to be effective, determined effort must be aimed toward the often distant future because, once a pattern is set, it requires even greater effort to reverse the trend. The mills of government grind slowly, but an essential factor in seeing they grind well is the challenge of free and educated citizens.

The Hobart Papers

Ten years after Professor Yamey's classic, IEA published the fiftieth Hobart Paper.[6] To mark this milestone, Arthur Seldon invited Professor T. W. Hutchison, an independent authority on the development of economic thought and policy, to appraise the contribution which the series had made "to a better understanding of the role of economic analysis in fashioning and criticizing public and business policy." In the resulting *Half a Century of Hobarts,* published in 1970, Professor Hutchison commended the series as performing

. . . the valuable service of keeping alive, against a tide of much influential current opinion, theories and ideas of great relevance for policy which had been temporarily submerged in this country not by any weight of empirical evidence and testing, but rather by dogmatism, fashion, and ideology.

On the impact of the Hobart contribution to public discussion of competitive enterprise, Professor Hutchison quoted a testimony from the opposing camp:

> . . . perhaps it is sufficient to point out that "even the ranks of Tuscany"—or the Fabian Society—have "scarce forborne to cheer." In a recent Fabian tract[7] it has been maintained that the Hobart series (and other IEA publications) "must be respected for the quality, consistency, and rigor of its approach to the treatment of private industry. . . . This is very far removed from a crude approach based on the vested interests of capitalists. . . . Its careful description of, and attacks upon, restrictive trade practices has been particularly impressive. . . . I concede a consistent and honorable attempt to remove a major blemish of the free market system."

The importance of such long-term educational efforts is that politicians and those who advise them have no time in office to think ahead in a coherent, much less objective way. Their dilemma has been described by Mr. Enoch Powell with characteristic force and wit:

> The supreme function of statesmanship is to provide against preventable evils. In seeking to do so, it encounters obstacles which are deeply rooted in human nature. One is that by the very order of things such evils are not demonstrable until they have occurred; and at each stage in their onset there is room for doubt and for dispute whether they be real or imaginary.

By the same token they attract little attention in comparison with current troubles, which are both indisputable and pressing: whence the besetting temptation of all politics to concern itself with the immediate present at the expense of the future. Above all, people are disposed to mistake predicting troubles for causing troubles and even for desiring troubles. "If only," they love to think. "If only people wouldn't talk about it, it probably wouldn't happen." Perhaps this habit goes back to the primitive belief that the word and the thing, the name and the object, are identical.

At all events the discussion of future grave but, with effort now, avoidable evils is the most unpopular and at the same time most necessary occupation for the politician. Those who knowingly shirk it deserve and not infrequently receive the curses of those who come after.[8]

For over two decades the IEA so far from shirking the discussion of "future grave but avoidable evils" has encouraged its authors to follow their argument wheresoever it leads them. The results have been such that no conscientious reader of IEA publications would be taken by surprise by the recurrent signs of the following "avoidable evils": the failure of the welfare state,[9] the collapse of the market for houses to rent,[10] the "land racket,"[11] road congestion,[12] the ineffectiveness of incomes policies,[13] the damaging aspects of EEC membership,[14] the misuses of trade union power,[15] the danger of a monetary explosion,[16] the coexistence of a record level of unemployment with an unprecedented rate of inflation.[17]

An independent university?

A last example of the effectiveness of the IEA's unique pioneering approach is provided by its publication in 1969 of an Occasional Paper entitled *Towards an Independent University* by Professor H.S. Ferns, a former socialist who had become disillusioned by the spread of state control, first in the Argentine under President Peron and then in Britain under Mr. Wilson. As the judgment of a political scientist, his opening paragraph commands special attention.

> For nearly three-quarters of a century more and more people of all classes and occupations have become more and more dependent in one way or another upon the state and have accordingly come under its control. It is now becoming increasingly obvious that this dependence and control are doing the community more harm than good, and that the moral and social energy of the people is diminishing through undue and prolonged entanglements in the web of government.
>
> The time has come to demonstrate on a large scale and in a sophisticated sphere of human endeavor and necessity that people on their own can meet a community need with no assistance from the state and entirely without state controls other than those designed to preserve the common law rights of individuals. To this end it is here proposed that an independent university be established for the provision of general higher education, the advancement of knowledge and the inculcation of habits of mental and moral discipline.

Professor Ferns drew on the shortcomings of the state-financed universities to show the advantages of such radical departures as full-cost student fees backed by a loan scheme, a general education in humanities and sciences taken together with European languages, the encouragement of more mature students, and the ending of life tenure and of uniform pay scales for university teachers. To show that wide support for this radical proposal existed among leading educationists, the paper by Professor Ferns included a declaration on "The Urgency of the Independent University" which by the time the second edition was published in 1970 was signed by 100 university teachers and headmasters. Some readers no doubt thought the idea academic in the sense of impractical. Yet within a year a planning board was set up under Sir Sydney Caine (a trustee of the IEA) and such progress was made that in 1973 it was succeeded by a fully-fledged Council for the University College of Buckingham. Having raised more than a million pounds, the council planned to attract further benefactions[18] to enable the college to open for its first entry of students in 1975.

In the concluding paragraph of *Towards an Independent University,* Professor Ferns clinched the case for this practical experiment in higher education by reference to a general proposition:

> If all knowledge is limited and uncertain, and all human beings and agencies make mistakes in their life strategy, the question is simply what arrangements will minimize the mistakes and maximize correct solutions.

Professor Ferns and all those who have helped carry his idea towards practical achievement answer that question by their actions.

On February 6, 1976, Buckingham University was inaugurated in the Town of Buckingham. Seventy-five students were enrolled. It was still short of money, but it was a valiant example of what can be done under difficult circumstances. I expect that it will thrive and be one of the best universities that the world has yet seen.

More private research needed

Although I have frequently been told that there is no other organization quite like the IEA, there are a number of groups in Britain and in America which have learned the advantage of putting their faith in scholarly research rather than political propaganda. On the other hand, there are a large and growing number of independent-looking research or educational bodies that are financed, partly or wholly and directly or indirectly, from public funds which must to some extent stop them from exposing all political prejudices to equal scrutiny and, where appropriate, equally uncompromising challenge. The fact that most economic "research" throughout the world is done by government, or financed from public funds, makes it all the more vital to strengthen genuinely private study financed by a diversity of business sources and foundations which, as Sir Miles Clifford (of the Leverhulme Trust) argued in 1970, "have more freedom to experiment, to share in adventure and search for new horizons than governments."[19]

In 1850 a Mr. Ellsworth, U.S. commissioner of patents, was invited to discuss the building of a larger block of offices for the patents division. He counseled caution because he felt that just about everything that could be invented had already been invented. Up to the time Ellsworth expressed this opinion 3,327 patents had been taken out and since then a further 3,000,000 have been registered.

A similar episode occurred when General Grant, as President of the United States, was given the opportunity of talking over one of the first telephone lines. Having satisfied himself that the apparatus worked, he sat back and said: "Yes, it is truly remarkable; but who in the world would ever want to use one of them?"

These may be amusing stories which indicate that the world has moved at a faster rate in the last hundred years or so than could have been foreseen. Yet had either Ellsworth or Grant possessed the power to decide what money would be spent on research and development, progress would have been stultified. So it is with economic research. My contention is that competition is just as much a discovery procedure in economics as in technical matters. The essential requirement is what Socrates called a private station, in other words an independent base such as the IEA, which makes it possible to avoid political pressures and compromise.

I could say much more about the success of the educational strategy first suggested to me by Hayek in 1945. There have been difficulties, especially in financing the steady growth of this backroom activity (without taking public subsidies or becoming dependent on any other dominant source). It has had to ward off people who wish to help, or sometimes hinder,[20] by mixing the IEA up with party politics. But there has been no shortage of first-class authors or of subjects to which their analysis can be applied. Nor have they been content with scholarly criticism but have gone on to offer positive proposals about ways of extending competition among suppliers and choice among consumers. Some proof of this intellectual pudding is provided in my concluding chapter which outlines a program drawing freely on what I have learned as a layman from IEA writers.

Since writing my first edition of this book, there have been many developments. In 1975 I was invited to Vancouver, British Columbia, to be a trustee of the newly formed Fraser Institute. My advice was sought in order to turn the F.I. into an IEA. Subsequently I became temporary acting director until such time as a Canadian could be found to do the job permanently.

The Fraser Institute published its first book on October 10, 1975, entitled *Rent Control–A Popular Paradox*. It was an updated version of the book on rent control published by the IEA in 1972. Dr. Michael Walker, the chief economist in Vancouver, proved himself to be an able editor and the publication, as of February 1976, has sold over 5,500 copies through the book stores and to universities and directly to students, making it, by Canadian standards, a best-seller. Press coverage has been extensive. By 1977, of fourteen new titles, four sold over 10,000 copies each.

Of the IEA, Patrick Hutber of the *Sunday Telegraph* of January 5, 1975, wrote: "Thank heavens for the Institute of Economic Affairs . . . what an incomparable debt we owe it . . . it has become the leaven in the whole economic mass. The center of useful economic activity is not to be found in the Treasury's economic section, not in the Bank of England, not presently in the universities, certainly not at the National Institute. More and more it is at Lord North Street, the institute's headquarters. . . ." And more recently Ronald Butt, in the *London Times* of January 8, 1976, has written, "The recent change of climate has been remarkable. Ten years ago the IEA . . . was still a bit of a joke. . . . Today, helped by the pressures of real life, it has shifted some of the best known economic writers in its direction and a good deal of the most influential economic thinking comes from economists published by the IEA. To most economists, the analysis of Hayek, Friedman, and other IEA authors has taken on a new relevance. . . ."

For reasons connected with the spread of political control and its accompanying high taxation, economists and others supporting the principle of reduced individual choice have had more research funds at their disposal than independent intellectuals like Hayek, Mises, or Popper, who have, even so, developed powerful arguments in favor of dispersed initiative and freedom of choice. I hope the examples I have given will encourage more people to study the neglected principle of maximizing choice as the way to escape from the syndrome of disaster which has developed in the wake of its opposite. If the full strength of the argument for choice has not yet come through what Hayek saw as the decisive intellectual debate, why should we expect legislation to move in that direction, except by chance?

As has been said of Christianity, the trouble with a policy to maximize choice in the modern world is not that it has been tried and failed, but that (with remarkable, perhaps temporary, exceptions like West Germany and Hong Kong) it has not yet been tried. It now provides perhaps the only hope of escape from more fashionable policies which have failed utterly, again and again.

6
What Must Be Done
A RADICAL PROGRAM FOR ECONOMIC REFORM

I have argued that the cause of the many social problems the world faces today, and has faced over many centuries, is lack of understanding of the natural laws or principles which govern human decision-making and human behavior.

I have attempted to indicate the right principles, demonstrating that the vast fund of human good intentions too often produces unsatisfactory, even self-defeating consequences, but that an application of better understanding can remedy the situation. We have seen how good intentions lead politicians astray because their actions are based on confused assumptions and are confounded by party politics which are increasingly irrelevant and harmful. I have applied this thinking to historical events and modern developments which appear to confirm my diagnosis. Having studied the predictable dangers that arise from false principles, I have emphasized what I see to be the relationship between sound theory and its practical application by governments.

The final application of my thinking requires the outline of an economic policy to implement it. This must be done without compromise, stating the objective and *likely* objections before setting down the program for action. If my approach is right and sufficiently well-explained, this document will produce consequences through its effect on readers and reviewers who in turn will influence the politicians.

Grim prospect

I am writing with the conviction that there exists a distinctive positive policy that would allow us to escape the syndrome that appears to be leading towards increasing economic and political chaos on an international scale. On the negative side, unless such a change is made in national economic policy, we will stumble in ever more unpleasant spasms down the steep slope of economic ruin. History, for those who care to read, is full of gloomy and frightening precedents.

Standards of living rose in spite of political ineptitude, and now are probably declining. Politicians have survived, though only just, by claiming credit for gains, but have increasingly been out of their depth.

What follows is an economic policy for prosperity. Although at first few may take heed, more will pay attention as things get worse. The aim is to achieve a transformation. We have every reason to expect that, like the German miracle, a dramatic improvement will begin soon after the policy of freedom is launched. Guided by our principles we may be astonished to find how little government intervention will be needed and how quickly an impossible position is improved.

The conditions under which any new British government is likely to find itself may be very grim indeed, and would include some, or all, of the following features:

1. a rapid decline in the value of money;
2. punitive taxes that cut into savings as well as take-home pay;
3. increasing taxes on things we buy;
4. multiplying price and wage controls;
5. increasing import and financial controls;
6. rationing and consequent black markets;
7. judges and courts unable to cope with all the offenders;
8. industrial strife, strikes, "rebellion";
9. growing threat of unemployment and trade stagnation;
10. political and economic weakness at home, leading to more troubles abroad;

11. an increasingly serious decline in the standard of living for more and more people.

It will be in the context of this vicious circle that the public will demand change. It is possible that the situation will be so bad that conventional politicians will claim more time and even try to delay an election. There may be demands for a coalition for "national emergency measures." Such a virtual dictatorship based on the discredited consensus would simply prolong the agony and delay the necessary changes.

Scope for choice

As politicians become less sure of themselves and less able to offer any alternative policy which has not already been discredited, many would wrongly welcome a coalition. The fashionable fear of not wishing to "abdicate responsibilities to the free market" will obstruct a move in the right direction. The international monetary crisis will reappear and "world bankers" will be exposed as emperors without clothes.

The compass bearing which guides my journey into the future is that, though the choice of each of us must be limited in certain specific directions, true wealth is created at the fastest rate possible under any given set of conditions when individual choice is deliberately maximized. It therefore becomes the duty of government to plan to maximize choice. This compass bearing will lead us to our destination, which I define as follows:

(a) the fastest possible rate of growth of wages and other incomes and therefore of the range of choice, *especially for poorer people*;

(b) arrangements to take care of the relatively few handicapped or incompetent individuals who are unable to fend for themselves, without obstructing the efforts of the most able on whom prosperity especially depends.

Low taxation and limited government expenditure are necessary for both these aims. In the crisis that is almost bound to come, many policies that have been thought politically impossible will at last have a chance to prove their effectiveness.

Signs of decline

Ever since the last war, politicians have made the British people feel a nagging sense of failure. Our national self-confidence has been sapped, we feel our problems are beyond solution, and complain of our lot in a way once thought the mark of less successful nations. It is no use blaming our decline on the loss of the empire. Britain was made neither great nor rich by the empire. We led the world before we acquired most of our colonies and it is a myth that we owed our wealth to exploiting them: our success was based on trade and enterprise on fair terms in all countries open to us, British or foreign.

Wealth and power were in any case only part of the foundation of our world influence, which rested also on the quality of British public life and political behavior. Our decline can be measured in a number of ways. Firstly, there is the reduction in individual freedom. Secondly, we see the growth of group envy and discontent, and the disappearance of respect for individual self-reliance. Success which comes from people's own efforts is resented while the idea of self-help and individual responsibility is attacked as anti-social by leading intellectuals. Thirdly, we appear unable to keep up with similar nations in economic growth. We are bottom of the league in the rate of economic growth among the world's developed countries. Whereas before the last war Britain had the highest standard of living in Europe, we have now been overtaken by all the other European countries except Austria, Finland, Spain, Portugal, Italy, and Greece. Although it is true that at present the margins are mostly narrow, other countries are moving ahead faster so that before long we will be among the *poorer* European nations unless we make a fundamental change of course.

These sad developments have gone along with our changed attitude to the state. We once regarded government as chiefly concerned with protecting peace abroad and order at home. Now we have come to look to the state as our universal provider. This attitude can lead only to poverty and tyranny (which will *not* be allayed by North Sea oil finds but rather by a radical change in policy).

A Summing Up

1. There is a basic principle fundamental to economic policy and it goes something like this: wealth is created fastest when individual choice is deliberately maximized.

2. It must therefore be the purpose of government to plan to maximize choice.

3. Governments almost inevitably begin *minimizing* choice to produce wealth. This paradoxical act must produce the opposite result and will end in devastation.

4. The thought given to economic principles is usually too late. But, as Dr. Samuel Johnson once observed, "If you know you are going to be hanged in a fortnight it concentrates the mind wonderfully."

5. It is possible to influence the future first by staying outside of politics and all vested interests, and then by documenting the right course to be taken and the consequences which will follow. The consequences arising from wrong policy should also be documented. The study and documentation of policy are in no way the same as taking part in politics, where compromise and vested interests are damaging.

There are several landmines in our way. The first is the desire to rush into politics. The difference between policy as such and politics is seldom understood. When Hayek told me that if I wished to have any consequences I must keep out of politics I think he may have been saying something more fundamental than he himself realized. I have discovered that Socrates would have given me the same instruction: ". . . He who will fight for the right, if he would live even for a brief space, must have a private station and not a public one." I emphasize the need for policy study because this must come first. All the evidence indicates that ideas do have consequences and are eventually reflected in political action.

The second landmine is the trade union problem. Unions in many countries (not of course dictatorship countries like the Soviet Union) have been given too much power and this presents a real problem. The fuse that sets off this particular landmine is inflation.

The third landmine is the misconception that confrontation or crisis by itself will automatically produce an answer. As we have seen all too clearly, the crisis does not necessarily produce the answer. Only intelligent premeditation and documentation can ensure that answer.

The fourth landmine is the assumption that the problem is only a monetary one. "Stop creating money by printing it and inflation will cease," they say. But they admit that there will be massive unemployment as the deflation takes place. They also point out that this is far better than hyperinflation, and here they are right because runaway inflation is totally destructive. But surely this is only part of the story. Certainly if governments are allowed to manage money at all they will mismanage it just as they have mismanaged everything else. To stop inflation, the government must not only stop spending and creating money, but it must get out of business. The government is not competent to offer services; it is only competent to make laws. There is abundant evidence that nationalized industries are unbelievably expensive and inefficient, and this includes schooling and hospitals. Stability is required, not inflation or deflation.

The fifth landmine is the mistake of trying to deal with what appears to be urgent rather than taking time to deal with the things that are vitally important.

The sixth landmine is the inevitable temptation to offer politically acceptable solutions on a temporary basis. This temptation, if yielded to, means that no one will ever hear the truth, neither politician nor public. The truth, insofar as we try to understand and explain it, is required for policy decisions, and nothing else will do.

Ludwig von Mises gives us this advice:

Everyone carries a part of society on his shoulders; no one is relieved of his responsibility by others. And no one can find a safe way out for himself if society is sweeping towards destruction. Everyone in his own interests, must thrust himself vigorously into the intellectual battle. No one can stand aside with unconcern; the interests of everyone hang on the result.[1]

Those who cannot or will not think may hide their heads in the sand. Others may try to build secret hideaways in such places as the Canadian tundra, arming themselves with dried foods and bars of gold. But for anyone with any intelligence there is only one way: thinking it through. And regrettably, thinking is the toughest endeavor to which man can apply himself.

People must come to realize that disaster is inevitable if we continue on our present course. I will be told that it is impossible to create such widespread awareness. I don't believe anything is impossible, provided we have the will to do it. I have only recently come to the conclusion that the warning process is absolutely vital. But warning that the economy will deteriorate is not enough. We have to warn of the total consequence, document it historically and theoretically. In the early stages we shall probably be shunned as maniacs or fools. In the end, when real trouble is at hand, people will listen.

I am saying, in brief, that the greatest requirement in the life of any of us, of our community or nation or world, is that we should start thinking before rank necessity overwhelms us. Voluntary thought is needed. We must study cause and effect and principles. This, in turn, means trying to think without prejudice, emotion, or vested interest.

A document announcing what the government should do in the near future is needed. I wish to suggest the following:

1. We should repeal all legislation that controls or restricts free ownership of property or the value of currency or foreign exchange.

2. The state should cease to play any role connected with money or coinage.

3. All controls on prices, wages, interest, and other interference with the market mechanism should be removed.

4. If collapse comes first, food must come before education. In that case, all schooling should find its own income. It will succeed in doing so: education is a valued commodity. Tuition will drop in cost as education enters the competitive market.

5. All capital taxes should cease at midnight. Governments should not be allowed to have one penny more than is necessary.

6. Since government expenditures would drop immediately, taxes could be cut immediately. All indirect taxes should be abolished overnight.

7. All legislation granting monopolies to any organization should be revoked. The state postal monopoly would necessarily disappear. Effective, competitive mail services would take its place.

8. All medical establishments should immediately raise their funds privately. They should be sold off or given away to private persons, charitable trusts, nonprofit or profit-making companies.

9. All unnecessary ministries or departments should be wound down and phased out, including health and education, which currently neither educate nor heal.

10. All foreign aid should cease: it frequently impedes fruitful capital investment in those nations that would benefit from it.

11. Old-age and other pensions should be phased out, and replaced by vested private pensions.

The consequences of this program should be understood. Immediately people will wish to work productively. They will be able to keep virtually all their pay and choose their own ways of living. The currency will strengthen at once, and stable prices will graphically demonstrate how much people have been cheated by inflation.

Immediately, the spurt in the economy will benefit those at the bottom. There will be jobs, less costly goods, and rising real wages. Company and individual profits will soar. Living standards will rise in real terms.

Those nations in the West that adopt such a policy will find themselves strong in every respect and able to resist the wiles of totalitarians. There is nothing between us and this happy condition but lack of understanding.

A Last Word

I have hammered away at my basic belief that the history of economic troubles repeats itself and does so not by chance or bad intentions but because some law of human behavior is not understood or applied.

Not bad men . . .

A recurring syndrome in history is that after a period of relative prosperity inflation develops, government takes more power away from individual consumers and producers, taxes increase, every failure of control leads to a further spread of bureaucracy, the value of money goes on dropping until the government resorts to some variant of wages and prices policy. Since such freezes or squeezes cause further pain without curing the original disease, they provoke even more serious political disorder.

Leaving aside the alibi of bad luck, and recalling that in Europe, as well as more recently in Asia and Africa, this recurring sequence has often concluded with a dictator who minimizes the choice of the individual almost to zero, the explanation could be that history periodically throws up people with evil intentions who enslave their fellow human beings in the guise of acting in the interests of the people and for the benefit of the working man. But seeing how well-intentioned politicians in Britain are heading the same disastrous way, I discount the possibility that bad men can generally be blamed for the syndrome repeating itself.

. . . but ignorance

So I conclude that the root of our troubles is the failure to understand logical cause-and-effect relationships. The distilled wisdom of the ages, which comes down from Socrates and other philosophers, has been expressed in the following aphorism.

He who knows not, and knows not that he knows not, is a fool; shun him. But he who knows not, and knows that he knows not, is wise; follow him.

I believe that the syndrome repeats itself because human beings act in ignorance and therefore in unconscious defiance of certain natural laws and principles.

If human beings are to convert good intentions into good results they have to study cause-and-effect relationships in economics—as has only relatively recently in man's history been done in the natural sciences. But in matters governing human relationships there is disagreement whether or not principles apply. Laws are made by government but, if no consistent cause-and-effect relationship exists, the outcome will not be as intended. I have provided abundant evidence that there is confusion on this subject and that, as an ordinary citizen faced with the consequences of bad government, I am entitled to say that many if not most experts have been proved wrong.

From principles to practice

In my attempt to define a possible fundamental principle, I have suggested that "wealth is created at the fastest possible rate when individual choice is deliberately maximized." Under such conditions the incomes and choices of the poorest will increase most rapidly. The reverse of this principle explains the failure of authoritarian governments, like those of the communists, which reduce choice and retard improvements in standards of living for the masses. It is necessary to emphasize that "choice-maximized" is not what is generally understood to be permissiveness. It does not mean that people can do as they please. It means that government is required to establish laws which maximize individual choice.

If there is a sound economic principle, how can we ensure it will be applied? I have tried to explain from history that, to be effective, well-founded understanding must be documented. This is an arduous exercise which is widely under-rated because thinking is regarded as less effective than action. Well-intentioned people almost invariably turn to party politics, lobbying, or demonstrations, which are too often forms of mindless action and so lead to the syndrome of failure and ultimately disillusionment.

There are many whose occupation is thinking. But these are mostly either academics who are often financed by governments and so influenced by prevailing ideas of what is thought politically possible, or politicians and civil servants who are responsible for the policies that have failed. It is unlikely that economists dependent on this establishment will uncompromisingly expose its failure and point to a quite different way ahead.

It can be done—again

From my study of history I contend that there is abundant evidence that the syndrome has repeated itself because of a general failure to understand that an unpleasant situation will be made worse by policies that reduce individual choice. Thus at its simplest, more controls and more taxes are applied in an attempt to undo the evils created by too much control and taxes. In contrast, there have been examples through the ages when governments have maximized choice instead of minimizing it, and prosperity has followed, sometimes on an almost miraculous scale.

I have studied some recent events which suggest that "choice-maximized" has produced prosperity and "choice-minimized" the syndrome. I have speculated that we can equate the benefits of broader choice with profits and the hardships of narrower choice with losses. As a rough guide, we can expect that when government expenditure reaches about half of the gross national product, losses may cancel out benefits and national growth will consequently slow down to zero. The measurement of voluntary as opposed to involuntary exchanges is not easy but it is apparent that inflation and high government expenditure go together. Both erode free choice.

Having provided some encouraging examples of the power of understanding when it is clearly documented, my final chapter applies the lesson by setting out a detailed program that would dramatically reduce government spending and put Britain, America, or any other country, back on the road to economic recovery and general wellbeing. Many, I am sure, will welcome my approach but may wonder if it disregards what is thought to be politically impossible. I invite each reader to study my case and make up his mind.

Notes

Chapter 1

1. Dictionary definitions of the word *principle* are: "A basic truth, general law of cause and effect" (*Advanced Learners' Oxford Dictionary*). "A law of nature by virtue of which a given mechanism etc. brings about certain results . . . a comprehensive truth or proposition from which others are derived . . . general truth forming a basis for reasoning or action . . . fundamental cause" (*Cassell*). "A primary element, force or law which produces or determines particular results" (*Webster*).
2. *Capital*, ed. F. Engels, Swan Sonnenschein, 1908.
3. *The Wealth of Nations*, Vol. 1.
4. *Ibid.*
5. Lin Yutang, *The Wisdom of Confucius*, Michael Joseph, 1958.
6. Some American writers have recently returned to the word *catallaxy* as preferable to *economy* in emphasizing the pervasive nature of exchange: Ludwig von Mises, *Human Action*, William Hodge, 1949. "Catallactics or the Science of Exchange" was first used by Whately in *Introductory Lectures on Political Economy*, London, 1831.
7. "On Liberty and Property," a lecture to the Mont Pelerin Society, 1958.
8. *The Road to Serfdom*, Routledge, 1944.

Chapter 2

1. *The General Theory of Employment, Interest and Money*, Macmillan & Co., 1936.

2. Arthur Shenfield, "Trial by Taxation," in *Right Turn,* Churchill Press, 1970.
3. *Reader's Digest,* May 1968, p. 176 (my emphasis).

Chapter 3

1. *History of Rome,* Vol. 6, Kegan Paul, 1883.
2. *The Common People of Ancient Rome,* Scribner, New York, 1911.
3. *A Relation of the Death of the Primitive Persecutors,* Amsterdam, 1687.
4. *The Social and Economic History of the Roman Empire,* OUP, Second Edition, 1957.
5. *The Fire and the Rose,* Collins, 1965.
6. This summary is based on a study published in *Innovator,* Box 3478, Los Angeles, Ca. 90034, U.S.A.
7. Ralph Myles Publishers, 1970.
8. Andrew Dickson White, *Fiat Money–Inflation in France,* Foundation for Economic Education, U.S.A., 1959.
9. *Hunger and History,* Caxton Printers, 1951.
10. "Hyperinflation in Germany," *The Freeman,* October 1970.
11. "The Great Depression," *ibid.,* October 1969.
12. *The Counter-Revolution in Monetary Theory,* Occasional Paper 33, IEA, 1970.
13. *The Millionth Chance,* Hamish Hamilton, 1957.
14. "A Tale of Two Railroads," *The Freeman,* September 1960.
15. *From the Tablets of Sumer,* Falcon's Wing Press, Indian Hall, Colorado, 1956; and *The Sumerians,* University of Chicago Press, 1963.
16. *Food Control During Forty-Six Centuries.*
17. *The Long Debate on Poverty,* Readings 9, IEA, 1973.
18. Institute for Humane Studies (unpublished paper).
19. United Nations Economic Commission for Europe, *Economic Survey of Europe in 1947,* Geneva, 1948.
20. W. H. Chamberlain, *The German Phoenix,* Hale, London, 1963, Ch. 2.
21. Ludwig Erhard, *Prosperity Through Competition,* Thames & Hudson, 1958, p. 12.
22. H. Morgenthau, *Germany Is Our Problem,* Harper, New York, 1945.

23. Erhard, *op. cit.*, pp. 10, 11, 13.
24. *Ibid.*, p. 13.
25. *Germany, an Experiment in Planning by the Free Price Mechanism,* Blackwell, Oxford, 1950.
26. *New Statesman,* December 1, 1956.
27. *Ibid.*, November 19, 1957.
28. Erhard, *op. cit.*, pp. 52, 69, 184, 228, 246.
29. *The Free Trade Proposals,* edited by G. D. N. Worswick, Blackwell, 1960.
30. "Will West Germany's Free Enterprise System Survive?," *Commercial & Financial Chronicle,* New York, June 14, 1962.

Chapter 4

1. A fuller account of the record of the MMB will be found in *The Marketing of Milk,* by Linda Whetstone, Research Monograph 21, IEA, 1970.
2. Speech to the Trade Policy Research Center, Waldorf Hotel, London, July 30, 1971.
3. *Wealth of Nations,* Vol. I, Book II, Chap. III.
4. *Goodbye to Nationalization,* Churchill Press, 1971.
5. *Right Turn,* Churchill Press, 1970.
6. *Paying for the Social Services,* Occasional Paper 16, IEA, 1967.
7. *National Superannuation and Social Insurance,* Cmnd. 3883, 1969, para. 25.
8. Published by Tom Stacey, 1970.
9. *Hansard,* January 27, 1959, cols. 993-4.
10. *Ibid.*, March 6, 1969, cols. 742-3.
11. Possible reforms are set out in *Down with the Poor,* Churchill Press, 1971, and discussed in more detail in Chapter 6 below.
12. The original findings were published in *Economic Journal,* December 1945; the words quoted are from Colin Clark's *Taxmanship,* Hobart Paper 26, IEA, 1964.
13. *Ibid.*, pp. 23-24.
14. *Local Government Finance,* Paper No. 2, Economic Study Association, 1971.
15. "Inflation and Wages," in *An Economist's Protest,* Thomas Horton, New Jersey, 1973.
16. *The Counter-Revolution in Monetary Theory,* Occasional Paper 33, IEA, 1970.

17. Reproduced with other essays in *One Man's View*, Churchill Press, 1973.
18. *Finance and Development,* IMF Quarterly, No. 4, 1970.
19. August 2, 1971.
20. July 16, 1971.
21. August 17, 1971.
22. Hodder & Stoughton, London, 1962.
23. "Europe and the Common Market," in the *National Westminster Bank Review,* February 1971.
24. September 20, 1970.

Chapter 5
1. *Reader's Digest,* May 1945.
2. "The Intellectuals and Socialism," *University of Chicago Law Review,* Spring 1949 (reprinted in *Studies in Philosophy, Politics and Economics,* Routledge and Kegan Paul, 1967).
3. Routledge, 1944, p. 69.
4. May 1, 1967.
5. The latest development in this sorry story was a report in the *Daily Telegraph* (November 1, 1973) that the government is being urged by the CEGB to allow American nuclear power plants (based on the light water reactor) to be built in Britain. The proposal was described as "a move which could kill the British nuclear development program."
6. Dr. Brian Hindley, *Industrial Merger and Public Policy,* IEA, 1970.
7. David Collard, *The New Right: A Critique,* Fabian Society, 1968.
8. Speech to West Midlands Area Conservative Political Center, Birmingham, April 20, 1968.
9. Harris and Seldon, *Choice in Welfare 1963,* and many other reports.
10. Norman Macrae, *To Let,* 1960.
11. Professor Donald Denman, *Land in the Market,* 1967.
12. Gabriel Roth, *A Self-financing Road System,* 1966.
13. Professor F. W. Paish, *Policy for Incomes,* 1964.
14. Professor J. E. Meade, *U.K., Commonwealth and Common Market,* 1962.
15. Professor B. C. Roberts, *Trade Unions in a Free Society,* 1959.
16. *Not Unanimous—A Rival Verdict to Radcliffe's on Money,* edited by

Arthur Seldon in 1969; and many other studies including Professor Friedman's *The Counter-Revolution in Monetary Theory,* 1970.

17. Professor F. A. Hayek, *A Tiger by the Tail,* 1972.
18. Although fees were fixed at a level to cover recurrent costs, the appeal was necessary to provide for scholarships and starting-up costs.
19. "Needed: Fair Play for British Charity," *Reader's Digest,* October 1970.
20. For example, by resorting to libelous words about the IEA, which on five occasions its legal advisers have required to be withdrawn.

Chapter 6
1. Ludwig von Mises, *Socialism,* Yale University Press, 1951, p. 515.

About the Author

Antony Fisher was born in London in 1915, educated at Eton and Cambridge, served in the RAF as a Battle of Britain pilot, and was awarded the AFC.

After a period in London he became a full-time farmer in Sussex, learned of the broiler industry during a lecture tour in the U.S.A., and in 1954 established the pioneering Buxted Chicken Company (later merged into Allied Farm Foods) which succeeded without government subsidy or protection in making record profits and dramatically reducing the price of chicken to the consumer. Mr. Fisher was a leading critic of the theory and practice of the British Egg Marketing Board from 1956 until it was wound up in January 1969.

In 1955 Mr. Fisher founded the Institute of Economic Affairs in London as an independent research and educational trust of which he is chairman of the trustees. In 1970 he established the International Institute for Economic Research in Los Angeles. He has lectured extensively in the U.S.A. and elsewhere on contemporary economic questions.

In 1974 he retired, turning over to his eldest son his dairy farming and other businesses.

He was invited to Vancouver, B.C., to be a trustee and temporary acting director of the newly-formed Fraser Institute, and then to New York to be a trustee and executive director of the new International Center for Economic Policy Studies.